"Said captures the essence of how projecting a positive mind-set—self-esteem, self-image, and self-worth—can create a vehicle to turn your dreams into your reality."

—DWIGHT HANSON
International Business Speaker and Trainer

"This is a book that will help you get focused on your success."

—TONY JEARY
The Results Guy, CEO coach

"A strong state is a strong economy. A strong economy is a strong business. A strong business is strong employees. Strong employees are an educated population. Financial knowledge is the foundation for the well-being of its people. To create your own financial knowledge, study this book."

—ASKAR SALYMBEKOV
Honored President of Dordoi Holdings

Me and
MONEY
THE PSYCHOLOGY OF WEALTH

Me and
MONEY
THE PSYCHOLOGY OF WEALTH

SAID
DAVLATOV

Clovercroft Publishing

Me and Money: The Psychology of Wealth

©2017 by Said Davlatov

Published by Clovercroft Publishing, Franklin, Tennessee

Interior Design by Suzanne Lawing

Cover Design by Debbie Manning Sheppard

Translated by Phillip & Olga Morrow

Edited by Tammy Kling

Copy edited by Gail Fallen

Printed in the United States of America

978-1-945507-66-3

Dear Reader,

What is your relationship with money?

Each of us has a specific way we feel and think about money, and we may not even recognize it. This book is designed to examine this relationship and the ways you can integrate a smarter money plan into your life.

The book you hold in your hands is based on experience from decades of trial and error. This is the process by which I've achieved success and have grown and built several successful companies. It contains knowledge given to me by my mentors, who have taught me so much. My mentors helped me to understand very important truths in life. They taught me to believe in myself and to overcome difficulties on the road to success. I hope I can do the same for you!

You may have picked up this book thinking that I was a multimillionaire with several people backing me from the start. The truth is, I was an average guy. I enrolled in and then dropped out of two universities because I could not afford them. If that's not discouraging, then I don't know what is!

It was a difficult period in my life because of where I lived. We faced war and the changes that followed afterward. Most people face a lot of adversity in life, yet war isn't one of them. Often the biggest challenge and war that we have is within ourselves. But the war I faced was real.

I started my life and business from scratch, and I faced many challenges along the way. There were failures and letdowns. Step by step, I gradually recognized my mistakes and learned from them. Have you ever experienced a personal failure and a great amount of learning from it at the same time? Sometimes, failure can be a gift.

I wrote this book with the intention of helping you avoid a lot of the mistakes I made and the obstacles I encountered. I sincerely hope that you will gain wisdom from this book and that it will help you believe in yourself and achieve your goals faster. If I can accelerate your success, you can achieve great things during your time here on Earth!

As you travel through life on your journey, I encourage you to remember the ones who inspired you along the way.

I want to thank the people who shared their invaluable experience—Bodo Schafer, who gave me the basis for my financial education, and M. S. Norbekov, who opened my eyes to the spiritual side of life. Humans are much more than mind and body. We are also spiritual beings with a heart and a subconscious and a soul, the essence of which is a large part of what drives many of our decisions.

Within my books, I describe the philosophy of the ant. The ant is an amazing creature from which we can learn a lot. Ants never quit. They will climb over or around or find another way if something obstructs the path to their destination. Ants always think ahead. They know summer doesn't last forever, so they constantly prepare for what comes next. The last important part of the ant philosophy is that they do not set limits. Think about it. How much food will ants gather to prepare for winter? All they can.

Can you apply the philosophy of the ant in your life? Absolutely!

1. Never give up.

2. Think ahead and plan for the future.

3. Do not limit yourself.

4. Do all you can do.

Let this book guide you on your way to success and prosperity. It will help you to understand yourself and think about who you really are.

A few of my goals in sharing my story with you follow:

- The book will help you to succeed in achieving your own success.

- The book will inspire you not to give up in difficult situations and will show you that you are not the only one who is facing problems or challenges.

Problems are universal. No matter your country of birth, nationality, status in life, or career—problems are universal.

It's human nature for people to exaggerate their own problems while marginalizing other people's problems. It's just the way we are! I want to encourage you today to realize that even though it may seem as if you have more obstacles to overcome than others, you don't. All successful people have encountered challenges in their lives.

However, the one trait all successful people share is that they believe in themselves. They are able to understand and learn from mistakes; recognize and apply the experiences of others to their own lives; and acquire the knowledge, manpower and resources necessary to succeed.

Most important, successful people always believe in success because they have confidence in themselves, and the future is half the battle.

The knowledge contained in this book is not a guarantee of your prosperity. Having knowledge is one thing . . . putting that knowledge into action is another. How many young people have a higher education, but do not know how to apply their knowledge in real life? Wisdom is applying knowledge to achieve results. Educated persons are not the ones who have diplomas. They are the persons who can take action and solve problems. They are the persons who can find solutions when others cannot or simply give up because it's too hard. They are the persons who believe in themselves and their future.

Education isn't a guarantee of success. Many "uneducated" people have gone on to start great companies or have taken the steps and have made the choices to create incredible lives. Education and knowledge aren't enough to live a successful life, and they won't guarantee results. You must be able to overcome stress, get up each and every day and do hard things, and make the right decisions . . . all in the pursuit of your dreams. When you make mistakes, you've got to be able to face them, overcome them, learn from them, and move on.

Another successful trait that high achievers share is preparation. Unless you lay the proper foundation, any great idea is bound to fail. Planning is essential for success.

You need to learn to plan your life. Those who do not plan the future must accept the fact that others are doing it for them. It is impossible to succeed without planning success. And remember, if you sow the seeds of poverty, do not expect the emergence of wealth.

As you read through this book, please know that I didn't start out a success. Don't be overwhelmed, and don't let those quiet voices in your head discourage you. If I can do it, so can you!

It is my hope that this book will help you improve your life and take you to a new level of success. I will pray, my dear reader, that you achieve your goals and realize your dreams. My highest wish is that you will pay it forward and share your achievements and knowledge with others along the way.

This is a different kind of book. As you turn these pages, you will realize that I've got a surprise for you. Within the book are the six basic secrets of financial freedom. They are scattered throughout the text. In order to find and understand them, you may have to read this book several times. Because only when your mind is ready will you be able to collect all these secrets, like a mosaic, in one piece. But you can be sure that I have already done half the work! Read, practice, and review, and it will be very easy. Take notes if you like, but make sure you begin to act immediately. And, with

God's help, success will come to you. Once you've learned the secrets to success, pass it on and mentor someone else.

All persons that I have met on my path of life are my mentors because they have shared a part of their experiences with me. My primary mentors are my students. Teaching is a two-way process. This book is a result of my seven years of teaching. Therefore, I express my deep gratitude to all the participants of my training that contributed to the creation of it. Many of my students used this knowledge effectively and have achieved success.

Good luck! Let this book help you achieve wealth and success, happiness and prosperity!

Sincerely,
S. Davlatov

CONTENTS

READER'S GUIDE FOR *ME AND MONEY*.... 16

INTRODUCTION 21

Chapter 1: WHERE TO BEGIN? 27

Chapter 2: TWO IMPORTANT LESSONS....... 39

Chapter 3: QUESTIONS ON THE
JOURNEY TO WEALTH............ 47

Chapter 4: HOW TO TREAT MONEY......... 51

Chapter 5: HOW TO SAVE.................. 81

Chapter 6: HOW TO INVEST 93

Chapter 7: HOW TO ENJOY MONEY 117

Chapter 8: OBSTACLES................... 127

Chapter 9: HOW TO MAKE MORE MONEY... 145

Chapter 10: PHILOSOPHY OF THE ANT 173

ABOUT THE AUTHOR 181

READER'S GUIDE FOR
ME AND MONEY

If you really decide to get rich, do not wait for tomorrow. Take action now. However, first ask yourself the question, "Are you ready to get rich?" After all, wealth is a way of thinking.

If you desire to learn how to think like a rich, successful person, then focus on a serious, meticulous, and interesting work. Start by reading this book, *Me and Money*.

Remember, this is not the usual kind of reading to which many people are accustomed. For a better understanding of the material, you have to constantly think about the content. Then you have to ask yourself questions, form opinions about what you read, and draw your own conclusions. You must use your power of imagination to place yourself in the position of the rich and successful people to feel their inner state.

Success, achievement, and any positive results are not possible without motivation. Your passionate desire to succeed will be the determining factor. Instructive books, inspiring movies, and professional advice will help you only if you strive for success. Constantly thinking about success and the ability to tune into success is important. After all, nobody can do it for you.

You should use a positive attitude as you pursue your success, which I hope this book will engender. Embrace the development of promising ideas, then build a detailed plan of action and implement it. Remember, the stronger the desire to succeed, the more opportunities you will find.

An ancient proverb says, "The desire—a thousand

opportunities, unwillingness—a thousand reasons."

Manage your emotions, use your positive qualities, and form good habits; use all of them to achieve success. Get rid of all your doubts. Focus on winning, thinking only about your dream, and do not let negative emotions influence your choice. After all, any success begins with a positive attitude.

Before you begin to read the book *Me and Money*, have four highlighters in different colors (green, red, blue, and yellow), bookmarks, and a notebook on hand. Keep them with you as you read. Use the green marker to emphasize the words associated with business, income, wealth, and money. Red means "no" (forbidden). It should emphasize the negative words that express doubt, fear, expenses, selfishness, bankruptcy, etc.

For example, in a sentence such as "Do not look for excuses for their poverty; otherwise the poor will always be," use red to emphasize the words "poverty" and "poor."

Use the blue marker to highlight wise sayings and words that define positive qualities—confidence, strength of will, commitment, determination, perseverance, etc.

Finally, use the yellow highlighter for keywords related to the basic rules, principles, and laws that you should follow in life. For example, in the sentence, "To be able to succeed, we must find a mentor who will show the way," highlight the words "find a mentor."

Try to plan your time so that every day you have the opportunity to find a quiet spot and devote at least forty-five minutes to reading this book. During this time, no one should interrupt you, and nothing should distract you from these serious lessons. Make arrangements with your loved ones beforehand so you will not be disturbed.

Each time, before you start reading a new chapter, take a few minutes to review the previous chapter. Remember that in school, each new lesson began with a review of the material previously covered. This is repetition. This principle will help you to learn and consolidate your knowledge, because your results will depend on it.

YOUR FIRST ACTION

You need a sort of "guide" which will help to identify the direction and consistency of your progress on the road to success. Start by looking at the table of contents. Note the words that seem important to you and that meet your inner mood. If something is not clear, write a question mark or an exclamation point in the margin. Do the same if you like some words in a heading. Use any icons that will make sense to you.

After you check all of your favorite words in the table of contents, scan through the book from beginning to end. Stop at all the titles of sections and chapters, as well as on the quotes of great people. If something draws your attention, mark it and underline it without hesitation, using your marking system. It is your personal handbook which you have to guide your own actions. Plan ahead: the more marks you make, the better they will help you understand the principles outlined here. This means that you will be able to use them in your life and achieve success.

YOUR SECOND ACTION

When reading books, constantly use the "Guide to Action," because in any journey a guide is needed, especially in the journey to the world of knowledge. It will guide you to the good roads and show you the way to your set goal. A guide will not lead you astray.

One of the basic rules of getting familiar with the book is to underline sentences, phrases, and even whole paragraphs that you find interesting and worthy of attention. Use special tabs for pages you want to return to. Prepare them in advance. Use the available space and page margins for making notes arising from thoughts while you are reading the book. If this is not enough space, you can use your notebook.

If you are already tuned in to the perception of information, you can continue reading. Do not rush to quickly finish the chapter. Read each chapter thoughtfully, without undue haste, and think carefully about what you have read. Then write down your thoughts and ideas that arise from your reading in your notebook. Your future depends on how well you understand the principles outlined in the book.

YOUR THIRD ACTION

In this book you will find six basic rules of financial freedom. They all operate in a complex fashion and are interconnected with each other. Study them carefully. Write down the most important things in your notebook, and refer to them in your actions. You must understand that an investment in knowledge is the most profitable, because it gives you an opportunity to earn thousands, or tens of thousands, of times more than you spend to purchase them.

I would encourage you to visit www.worldpreneur.com to join our online community of world changers, interact with our renowned authors and speakers, and download additional content related to *Me and Money* and other publications.

INTRODUCTION

Great opportunities come to all,
but many do not know they have met them.
~ALBERT DUNNING

When you read this book, try to forget about your daily cares and concentrate on serious reading. To begin, ask yourself this question: do you want to be rich?

If you just want to earn more money, then this book is not for you. However, if you have big dreams, and if you know exactly what you are striving for, this is the book for you!

You can achieve wealth and abundance.

I often meet people who talk about their desire to be rich. I have also met those who consider themselves to be rich. I have met people who shrug and tell me, "Yes, if I wanted to, I would have already become rich!" There are people who have decided that they don't desire a lot of money because it is not the most important thing in life for them. But very rarely have I met people really ready to become rich.

After reading this book you will have two choices: (1) to make a decision and start acting or (2) do nothing, and leave everything as it was. Yes, even after reading this book, you will not necessarily get rich. However, in my opinion, you will never forgive yourself if you do not use the knowledge gained

SAID DAVLATOV

from this book.

It is one thing if a person does not know and therefore does not act. It is quite another thing if a person does know and still does not act.

To get started, I would like you to think about this question: what traits enable you to become rich?

How many answers can you think of? Ambition, determination, a strong will, ability to earn . . . these are all good traits. But here is the most important definition to know: rich persons are persons who have their money working for them. They are not working for their money. It is important to understand, accept, and remember this definition—rich persons are persons who have their money working for them.

Now let's try to imagine a way of life of someone rich. Or picture yourself as wealthy, and then answer the following question: what would I do if I had a lot of money? To visualize this, get a pen and a piece of paper.

Take eight minutes and write down all the things that you would do if you were rich. Imagine that you have so much money that cost does not matter. Write down everything that comes to mind, without stopping, preferably without taking pen from paper. When you stop to take a break, you will have written about everything that is missing from your life at the present moment.

These are not your dreams or goals. This is what is missing from your life. Only after this step will you begin to record the goals you really want to achieve. And you will see your dreams take shape. They will be much clearer to you. It is very important to remember to be peaceful and intentional about your attitude and mind-set. Feel like a successful and happy person, and write.

When you have finished writing, count how many pages you have written. One, two, three? Personally, I have twelve pages.

The first time I completed this exercise, my mentor said that he did not want to teach me. He said that I did not have any dreams, although I thought I had written about very important things. He shifted my thinking and encouraged me to dream bigger.

Do the exercise again; only this time do it a little differently. Now try to record your wishes in a relaxed environment, and slowly and carefully think things through. The process of reflection and meditation is like walking through the forest. If you go once, you do not leave any trace. After two to three times, the signs will be visible, but, nonetheless, they will eventually disappear. When you pass through ten times, you will leave a trail.

What you are thinking about right now? Can you imagine that these are only your first steps? You are just starting to create your own path on the way to wealth.

As we travel together on this journey, I will encourage you and explain the steps. The more you walk through the process, the more you will begin to understand. Patterns will begin to form in your mind.

All of this can be explained from a scientific point of view. Our brain is made up of eighty-six billion neurons. Each neuron is responsible for a particular action or concept. If you hear the word "home," you think of your home. If you read "red house," then you will think of a red house, most likely a red-brick house. In this case, the neuron responsible for the word "red" is connected to the neuron responsible for the word "house." If you repeat this combination over and over again, it will create a stable connection of neurons, a stable image (like a stencil). Next time, just hearing the word "house" will cause you to picture a red house. This is basically how patterns of behavior are formed.

Therefore, if you think of yourself as a rich person and behave like a rich person, then you will begin to think like a rich person.

If rich persons lose all their wealth and all their money, six months later they will be rich again. If you give a poor man a lot of money, in six months he will become poor again. This is because both poverty and wealth are an internal state, a way of thinking, and a way of life.

This is very important to understand. The rich have a special way of thinking. Even though they have a lot of money, the rich do not stop working. The words "I am so tired, so tired! If I had money, I would rest" are the words of a poor person. Rich people have an abundant mind-set. Rich people are enthusiastic about work.

Many people say, "I have a lot of ideas, but no money. I am very smart and very talented, in fact almost a genius. If I had money, I could do a lot. But I do not have money, and therefore I am powerless." It does not matter how intelligent you are or if you are actually a genius; if you do not apply yourself or have the right mind-set, nothing in your life will change.

Persons with a poverty mentality often make the choice not to change. When they are told, "If you act and do something, then there will be money," they reply, "What can be done without the start-up capital? First, you give me the money, then I will act, because it will not work without money." I do not have to even ask what kind of business it is. These people are convinced that in order to do something, to achieve something, they need money. And a lot of it. However, in my experience, the most successful people say just the opposite. Successful people say, "Even if I have nothing, I will make things happen. Just watch me."

Study the lives and achievements of those who have succeeded, and use that knowledge to help yourself. Follow the rules and principles that successful people have developed. Do that, and in two to three months you can increase your income by 30 to 70 percent.

You can acquire the knowledge you need by reading this book. You will have the chance to realize your dreams. Develop an "anything is possible" mind-set before we begin. I am in this with you.

First, you have to examine your mind-set. What is your relationship with money? Do you think there is only a little love, a little money, or a little luck? If you think that way, you have a limiting belief, a limiting mind-set, because all of these things are available in abundance. The main thing is to be able to acquire them.

Some of what you will learn by reading this book may conflict with your beliefs. It may seem wrong to you. However, if you really want to achieve your goals and turn your dreams into reality, you need to tune in to the training. You will need to be open to the possibility that you have held limiting beliefs for a long time and that now is the time to remain open to change.

Your task will require awareness, understanding, and a positive perception of the new information.

Today is the day.

Let's get started.

CHAPTER 1

WHERE TO BEGIN?

Control your own destiny or someone else will.
~JACK WELCH

Some people believe that creating massive wealth requires a big, bold move. But managing anything in life begins with managing something small. If you can take care of yourself and the small things in your life, you can take care of others. If you can take care of a small amount of money, then you can manage a larger amount.

First you need to learn how to manage a small amount of money.

Until you learn how to manage small amounts, you cannot manage large amounts. According to statistics, sixteen out of every one hundred people will become wealthy, but only one of those sixteen will preserve their wealth for the rest of that person's life. Only that one person will be recognized as being wealthy.

Why is wealth so difficult to accumulate?

Without a doubt, money is easy to get. However, it is easier to earn money than to save it.

Remember the main rule for those who desire to become rich: *Put your capabilities higher than the money, and then the money will come to you and will serve you.* If you put your capabilities below the money, then the money will determine what you eat, what you wear, where you go on vacation, and what to give to loved ones. Put your capabilities higher than the money, and then you determine the quality of your life. Read this rule a few times and think about it. You need to learn it and repeat it often.

Do you like your job?

In order to achieve something, you need more than a little love for what you do. You need to have passion. A passion that will drive you even if you have to experience pain should something go wrong.

Not everything you do will work out right the first time. Passion will keep you focused on your dream.

There are people who have given up on their dreams. They no longer have any passion. These people are the ones who only do what is needed. They are merely working for a paycheck.

They arrive to work on time, accurately perform their duties, and leave on time. However, the passion is not there. It is much more important for them to be in the process. They are only going through the motions to get a paycheck. These people no longer dream. Their end result is that they achieve nothing. If you want to become rich, never be the "person in the process."

A person in the process is either driven by the process or by the fear of never having enough. Fear can cause the death of your dreams. If you fear that you will never have enough or never be good enough, you will stay where you are for the rest of your life. Confidence in your dreams aligned with action will bring you results.

No one is responsible for your prosperity. Let me repeat, no one is responsible for your prosperity.

It is not the government's job, your family's job, or even your spouse's job to take care of you. You are responsible for yourself. To achieve your goals, you need to develop a different outlook, a different experience, a different pattern of thinking.

The first time I came to Moscow, it was just to relax, see the city, and visit Red Square. When my money ran out and I needed to go back home, I arrived at the train station and tried to persuade the conductor to let me on a train even though I had no money for a ticket. I explained my situation and offered my passport as collateral, but he refused.

Now I am so grateful to the conductor for his stubbornness and for refusing my request. If I had left, everything would be different.

There, at the station, one person talked with me. I explained the situation I was in. I told him that I came to see Moscow, had spent all my money, and could not afford to go back home. In response, he laughed and said, "You know, people from many countries come here without money, earn money, and then leave. You came with money, and you want leave without money, but you cannot." It is very important to listen and really hear very important words. God, for sure, will say what to do through someone. Pay close attention.

I replied that I was ready to do any work, but where could I find it?! He laughed again and told me, "Moscow is the big city. Many people come here and work—Afghans, Vietnamese, Koreans, Chinese—not including visitors from the former Soviet Union. You say that you cannot find a job here?! It is not true."

I started thinking and realized that he was right. In that

moment, I promised myself that I would not go home until I earned a decent amount of money.

I found a suitable job fairly quickly and started to work, tirelessly.

To save the most money, I tried to cut back on everything. I was successful in setting the money aside, but I did have roadblocks. I was an immigrant without a work visa.

One day, the police took almost all the money I had managed to save. They took advantage of my powerless position since I did not have the right to say anything about it. I had almost nothing left. There was no one to complain to, and it did not make any sense. I had to start over again, to work, to cut back even more, and save. However, the story repeated itself again and again. It was very disappointing. I didn't know what to do. The total amount of money taken from me by the police added up and was quite significant at the time.

After the last incident with the police, I was completely broke. I was desperate. I felt hopeless. I had nowhere to go. One morning, I got on the subway and headed towards the Kiev railway station. I got off at one of the stops and walked along the Moscow River. I sat down on a bench and began to pray, "Lord, why is this happening this way? Why me? I am a hardworking man, doing honest work. Why can't I achieve the lifestyle that I dream of? It's so unfair." I prayed and cried.

It was then that I began to change my mind-set, my worldview. It was a revelation. I looked at myself. I had wet shoes, dirty clothes, and was filthy and unshaven. I had lived on the streets for three months trying to raise money to go home. Did I really dream of such a life?

Then I heard my inner voice, as if God decided to answer me, "You did have the money, but you could not manage it. You could have spent it wisely and lived better, but you did not do so. You've dreamed of getting an education. Not only did you not go to school; you were also wearing yourself out working, not taking the time to rest. That's why I took your money."

This was an incredible voice, an incredible revelation. Pay attention to what you hear. It is such a moment that can be a turning point in your life. In that moment, it came to me. I understood why people who worked eighteen to twenty hours a day never become rich.

I remembered my uncle. He wore himself out working. He would get up before light and lay down after dark, but nothing changed in his life. Someone in his family was always sick. Something was always broken. He was always working tirelessly to fix a problem. Nothing ever changed for him and his family because they never tried to do things differently. To them the situation was the best it could be. What if they had decided to do things differently?

Maybe you are stuck in the same place. If you need to make a change, today might be the day. We are equipped with mind, body, and soul. Use what you have been given and be confident that you can make a change.

There is nothing more perfect than the human brain, but we need to learn how to use it. We have to be willing to think differently.

Ninety-eight percent of people think in the old, well-established stereotypes, and that's it. They are our relatives, friends, and acquaintances. Everyone has said something like this, "If I had the money, I would start a business. But I have no money, so I can't do anything."

The truth is, the rules of getting rich are simple. To get rich, you must act. To realize your dream, you need to change your way of thinking.

Ask yourself this. Do people get rich first and then become smart, or are they smart first and then get rich? Of course, the answer is "smart first, then rich." Learn from the rich and successful people. Most important, use the knowledge you gain to shape your passions towards your dream, your work, and yourself. Then start taking action.

If you want to become rich, never be the person in the process. Be the person who gets results. To understand this a little better, consider the following story.

STORY OF "IMAGINING THE SOLUTION"

On a cold and foggy day, two boys went skating on a frozen lake. The ice was not thick all over; however, the kids did not pay any attention to it. Suddenly the ice cracked, and one of the boys fell in. He was sucked under the ice. The other boy remained calm, grabbed a rock, and with all his strength, began to beat on the ice. He smashed through it and pulled his friend to safety.

When rescuers arrived and saw what had happened, they asked, "How did you do it? The ice is thick; it was impossible to break it with a rock and those little hands!"

At that moment, the group was approached by an old man. Smiling, he said, "I know how he did it."

"How?" they asked him.

"Nobody was here to tell him that it was impossible."

Have you ever done anything that seemed impossible?

Walt Disney said that if you can imagine it, you can do it. Disney created a theme park from his imagination. If he could do that, imagine what you could create! Anything is possible.

ACTIVATING YOUR CAPABILITIES

One can know his abilities only
when putting them into practice.
~SENECA

We can learn a lot about finding out about one's capabilities from the parable of the crocodiles.

There lived a rich man who had a very beautiful daughter. The rich man wanted her to get married. However, he was concerned about her. Would the suitors be interested in her or her father's wealth? So he decided to test the suitors. He brought the eligible young men together and told them, "Whoever makes it through the pool first will get to choose: one-third of my land, one-third of my money, or my daughter's hand in marriage. However, you should know there are a dozen crocodiles floating in the pool."

Before he could finish the warning, one young man was in the pool. The rich man was surprised. He wondered about the courage, the will, and the determination this young man possessed. Crocodiles rushed after him, but he was swimming fast! As they tried to catch him, the brave young man swam even faster. Finally, he climbed safely out of the water on the other side of the pool.

The rich man asked the young man if he wanted one-third of his land.

"No," the young man replied.

The rich man asked, "Do you want one-third of my money?" He got the same reply.

"No."

The rich man was pleased and asked a final question, already sure of a positive response. "Do you want to ask for my daughter's hand in marriage?"

The young man again replied, "No."

Puzzled, the rich man asked, "Then, what do you want?"

The young man said, "I want that bastard who pushed me in the pool!"

This example shows that not all people can correctly assess their abilities, either physical or intellectual. However, in an emergency these underlying capabilities reveal themselves.

The young man would never have jumped into the pool voluntarily. But since the young man was already in the pool, he accomplished something that he did not know he could.

A good mentor will help you do things you would never do voluntarily and can help you discover your abilities. A bad mentor will say, "Well, you can do it tomorrow." That is not love; it is pity. A surgeon can pity a fatal complication. That's what you need to remember.

RULES OF THE RICH

Imagine you are already in the pool with crocodiles. In a figurative sense, the "pool" may be your finances, your world of money. And you can survive only with your ability to manage money. To do this, it is necessary to know the principles of money and understand the laws of financial management.

To get started, remember a few basic rules rich people use in their lives.

First, the goal is not to have small dreams or own material things. The goal is to find the dream that ignites your passion and makes you act.

Second, money reacts to events and behaves as humans do: treat it well, do not push it away, and it will come to you and remain with you.

Third, those who do not plan their future must accept the fact that someone else will plan the future for them.

Fourth, what we have comes from what we do.

Remember these rules: apartment, car, house, electronics, jewelry—they are not the goal. We will come back to them.

Why do we talk about money or of wealth? Because it matters! Remember the story about the pool with crocodiles? We must learn how to manage money. No matter how small or how large. Everyone—no matter if you are a spiritual person or even if you are a monk—has to think about money sooner or later. Why? Because it drives the world, and it can make or break your life.

If you have no money, no one will care about your degree, your work, or your brilliance. If you cannot afford to fly to the job interview, how will you achieve success or change the world? Even if you have a higher education but no money to help others or travel to a friend's wedding or live comfortably, then even your PhD is worthless. Eventually this lack of planning will lead to embarrassment.

Just think, one day you will be able to earn more in a single day than you have earned in all your previous years. It's like a sporting event. To win the competition, which lasts only minutes, the athlete trains for months and years. The audience may look at him and think that the success came to him at that moment. But that's not true. Success is a series of repeatable actions. It is a compound effect of choices you make every day which result in repeatable actions that create healthy and successful habits. All it takes is the right frame of mind and the right way of thinking.

Success is the result of long and diligent training combined with working every day on the path toward your goals and dreams. And if you consider yourself worthy of the lifestyle you dream about, you have to learn to manage money.

For most people, money is a source of stress. At the beginning of the book, I asked the question, "What is your relationship with money?" Remember that every relationship is built on emotion, and your relationship with money is no different.

As you embark upon this journey to learn about money, keep a positive mind-set. Stay happy! Examine your feelings about money.

First, I want to tell you a remarkable story;

A little girl ran to her mother and asked, "When you grow up, do you become someone?"

Her mother did not hesitate and answered, "I became a

woman."

"Mom, why did you lie? You *are* a woman," the daughter replied. "Tell me, when you're older, do you become someone?"

"I'm a teacher," her mother said.

"You have always been a teacher!" the daughter cried in surprise. Then she repeated her question. "Mom, who do you become when you're an adult?"

The woman finally realized that to her daughter, she had always been a mother and a teacher, but that was not enough for her daughter. In that moment, the woman felt she could have achieved more success, been more significant. The woman saw the desire for more in her daughter's eyes. After all, children dream of seeing their parents in the title role and not in the background. Remember that children, too, want to be proud of their parents.

Notes

_____

_____

_____

_____

_____

_____

_____

_____

_____

_____

_____

_____

_____

_____

_____

_____

_____

_____

_____

_____

_____

_____

_____

_____

CHAPTER 2

TWO IMPORTANT LESSONS

Students are more willing to seek the one who shows the way,
and not the one who explains the error.
~ QUINTILIAN

Here are two important lessons for any person who wants to succeed.

First, where there is a good success, there is always a mentor. No matter how educated and intelligent you are, a mentor is essential. The mentor will shorten the way to your dream, help you avoid common mistakes, and teach you money management.

Second, if you want quick success, watch the people who are where you want to be, financially and in your career. This will help you to quickly find a mentor. If you are observant, within a week you can identify a number of individuals who match your criteria and then select the appropriate mentor.

When I first met Bodo Schafer, here's what struck me, what made me decide to change my life. He asked me a few questions that made me think and we talked a little bit. Then he said: "I've been wondering, why did you decide not to be rich?"

He did not ask me if I wanted to become rich or if I knew how to get rich. No, he asked me why I was still not rich. He pointed out that the questions he asked me were the same questions his mentor had asked him. Here are the five questions.

1. How long can you live off your savings if you suddenly lose your job or source of income?

_____

_____

_____

_____

Think about all of your general expenses: food, clothing, utilities, transportation, etc. Divide the total amount of your savings by your total monthly expenses. This will give you the number of months you can live off your savings right now. Your answer is the result of your life up to now. If you are not pleased with the result, you should reexamine your attitude toward work and the distribution of income.

Money gives you a much different feeling than having things such as a car, electronics, jewelry, and other household items. Unless you do not have money, you would not even consider selling your car; that would never come to mind.

If you have money, you will feel more confident and free.

However, most people's answers on this issue are not encouraging. After working for many, many years, the majority have nothing to show for their years of hard work. I travel to different countries to work and teach so that my students, even at an advanced age, can afford to live happily and help their families.

My mentor told me, "I started at the bottom and achieved a high level of success in my life. I don't want you to do the same and start from scratch. It is better to take my knowledge, my experience, and use them. Start at the higher level and do not stop on the level that I achieved. Keep moving forward. Life should always be rich and interesting."

2. Have you set aside enough money? Do you think you could save more?

_____

_____

_____

_____

If you believe that the money you have set aside can ensure your financial future, then answer yes. If you think that you do not have enough money saved, then the answer is no. In either case, you have to think very carefully about your financial situation and what you can do to ensure financial stability for your future.

3. Do you have a financial plan?

_____

_____

_____

_____

Many believe that the basis for success is a good financial plan. If you have a financial plan, that is good. I also had a financial plan; however, it was a plan for how to spend money. I had not yet received the money, but I was already planning how to spend it. The plan looked something like this.

What will I buy?	When will I buy it?
Leather jacket	Two weeks
Washing machine	One month
Furniture	Three months
Training program	Five months
Flat screen TV	Seven months
Home improvements	One year
Car	Two years
Engagement ring	Three years
Wedding	Four years

I thought it was a good financial plan. The money had not yet appeared, and I had already spent it. The majority of people have this type of plan. Then they wonder about their money and where it went, saying, "I earned a lot of money, but where did it all go?" They have one plan and that is how to spend.

In reality what they need is a plan on how to multiply the money, increase revenue, and manage expenses wisely.

Believe me, it is better to spend three to five years consciously managing money and limiting expenses than to live a lifetime in financial hardship. When you do this, you are making great strides towards wealth and can then live the rest of your life as you want. Bodo Schafer told me, "In five to seven years—well, for most, in ten years—you will be financially free."

I was financially free in three years. I was doing twice as much as I was asked to do and what I had planned to do myself.

Always remember the words of Jesus. In Matthew 18:22, Jesus said, "I tell you, not seven times, but seventy-seven times."

Imagine the results we would have if we thought the same way. I followed this example. If I was given a job, I did twice as much as what the teacher advised. If the teacher said to do it once a day, I did it twice. This helped me to achieve my goals in three years.

Implement this principle towards your goals, and you will succeed. We are who we believe ourselves to be.

    4. Can you foresee a time when you live on the interest of money you have invested?

_____

_____

_____

_____

This is the time when your money works for you . . . revenues exceed expenses, and the remaining funds are invested.

Think about the answer and write your statement. Turn on your imagination and think positively.

    5. Do you get as much as you deserve?

_____

_____

_____

_____

This is a very powerful, thought-provoking question. Some will answer yes. Some will say no; they deserve more. There is hope that if you really want it, you will get it, and then you will make changes in your life for the better. If you think you can earn more, please go and earn more. The main thing to decide for yourself is what you are capable of, and that will help you achieve your goals and live the lifestyle you dream of.

Really think about it . . . these are the five main questions that will help you understand your current situation. Often someone's own personal obstacle or blind spot regarding money is linked to an event in his or her life or childhood. If a parent lost everything or declared bankruptcy, there may be a fear or hesitation around money. If a person grew up poor, there may be a poverty mentality.

In order to grow, you need to reflect on your past, rethink the present, and define the main objectives for your future. To help you do this, try to answer a few additional questions.

6. Would the quality of your life be better if you earned more?

_____

_____

_____

_____

7. What would happen in your life, if you were working at full capacity? Would your quality of life be better than it is now?

_____

_____

_____

_____

Be thoughtful about your answers and then decide. Do you want to make things easier in your life? The answer is no; you want to try to make your life better. The easy path does not lead to big goals.

Do you want fewer problems? Again, the answer is no. It is better to improve your skills while you are overcoming obstacles. You will encounter problems. If you learn to master them, it will be a result of solving the problems that you faced. They will have made you smart. Even raw gold goes through fire to become pure gold. This is the law of life. Many people know these things; however, nothing in their lives changes.

They do not want to change anything because they are satisfied with poverty or they have learned to live with it.

All that you achieve in this life is the result of hard work to overcome obstacles.

Notes

CHAPTER 3

QUESTIONS ON THE JOURNEY TO WEALTH

A person with a clear purpose will make progress, even on the roughest road. A person with no purpose will make no progress, even on the smoothest road.
~THOMAS CARLYLE

Everyone should understand these five main concepts—the answers will lead you to wealth.

1. How to treat money.

2. How to save.

3. How to invest.

4. How to enjoy money.

5. How to make more money.

Remember, in order to become rich, you must first learn

how to manage a little money and to think like rich people do. People are smart first, then rich. Rich people do not work for money, but instead work to master a skill.

Having become masters, they enjoy their work. They have developed a passion for their work . . . enjoyment that only masters can receive from their work. Do you know what even death cannot take away from us? What remains with us forever? It is our skill and our dignity since they are always with us.

Therefore, if you take away rich persons' wealth, they will be rich again in a few years. After all, even after losing their fortune, they retain their knowledge, skills, ability, thinking, etc. They still possess all the things that made them rich in the first place.

There is a cautionary tale about the ancient Greek philosopher Bias. When the Persian King Cyrus besieged the city of Priene in Ionia and was ready to seize it, the people began to leave the city. They were carrying the most precious of their possessions. Only Bias came out taking nothing with him.

Surprised by his action, the citizens asked Bias, "Why do you leave empty-handed?"

The philosopher replied, "I carry all my effects with me," referring to his knowledge, which was much more important than material wealth.

Later, many of his fellow citizens lost their property. Even worse, they did not know how to earn a living. Bias, who was considered one of the seven sages, taught people lessons. Then, with the money he earned from teaching, he fed some of his fellow citizens. His words, "I carry all my effects with me," became a popular expression.

Life is complex. We cannot easily separate money from everyday life and everything that surrounds us. Yet money is still not an indication of wealth. There are people and they are certainly rich. However, simply looking at the person's face, you may not see the expression of joy and happiness. You cannot see "rich." Answer this question: "Why do you want to be rich?"

There must be a reason. This reason is related to the purpose of your life. You can answer the question by writing it down. Please try to avoid general statements such as "Who doesn't want to be rich?" or "Everyone wants to be rich!" Your answers should reflect your inner mind-set, your dreams, and your attitude towards life. The answers are yours and yours alone; you own them. They are unique and individual to you.

NOTES

_____

_____

_____

_____

_____

_____

_____

_____

_____

_____

_____

_____

_____

_____

_____

_____

_____

_____

_____

_____

_____

_____

_____

_____

CHAPTER 4

HOW TO TREAT MONEY

Wealth is power. With wealth, many things are possible.
~S. Clason

It is impossible to consider money separately; you need a reason why you want to be rich. Now answer this honestly. What is your attitude toward money? Does money help you survive, or does it simply give you the opportunity to live well? Does money corrupt? Does the lack of money cause problems in your life and in your family? Everyone has his or her own opinion.

Remember what we heard when we were young? "Money is the root of all evil." Have you have seen many movies where the rich man was good? Most people grew up in a community where there were not many rich people. Sometimes there was someone who was a bit wealthier than others, but was not really rich.

Some people wanted to be wealthy at all costs, and other

SAID DAVLATOV

people were afraid to have a lot of money. If you had two bikes, a luxury car, or other nice things, some people looked down on you or were jealous of what you had.

Times have changed, but the consciousness of many people has not yet adapted to the new way of life. They think, *Why would I want a lot of money?*

A lot of money can bring misery to such a family. They remember the examples of where wealthy people were involved, their family life was miserable. Or they focus on raising a happy and healthy family, and they simply do not see themselves as wealthy persons at all. Wealth is not their goal or dream. They do not believe wealth is attainable.

Sometimes this information works on a subconscious level, whether we like it or not. There are some people who want to become rich, but unconsciously drive away money. A believer can say, "Someone who is rich does not get to heaven. I may not be rich, but I'm a good, honest man. Look at the rich people. They get into politics, violate laws, deceive people, and steal from the people."

This reasoning is incorrect. In the world there are a lot of people who are rich and are still good people.

The truth is, not only are you worthy of being wealthy; it is a good thing if you become wealthy. You will be able to do more, be more, and give more. Think of the people you could help if you were wealthy. Think of the dreams you could achieve if you were wealthy. You are worthy of being rich and worthy of the lifestyle you dream about.

Think of it this way. You have five fingers on each hand. You do not think that one finger is more important than another, do you? We can agree that all of your fingers have the same value. Now look at your hand and spread your fingers apart. Let's assign each finger something that's important for everyone.

First finger: This represents your family and their well-being. Your family should always be provided for; otherwise, you

52

will worry and lead a stressful life.

Second finger: This represents your health. If you take care of yourself and live a healthy lifestyle, you will be happy and enjoy your life more.

Third finger: This represents money. Money is just as important as your health and family. Some people spend their health first to make money. Then they spend money in an attempt to restore their health. And that's how their life ends.

Fourth finger: This represents your self-worth, or sense of self. Being self-aware means you understand yourself and know what you feel about yourself at any given time in your life. The states of your health, your mood, your mind-set, and everything in between all impact you. Usually, no one pays attention to self-awareness. To feel good, you need to determine exactly who you think you are in this life. How do you see yourself? How do you feel? Then you can ensure that every day can be productive. Productivity and happiness go up when a person is in a good mood. When things go well, everyone in the family will be happy.

Fifth finger: This represents your purpose in life—the meaning and drive you have and what is most important for you to accomplish. This purpose is what drives you to get out of bed each day and move forward.

All of these things are equally important. There are people who think career comes first and then marriage. Or marriage first, then career. Others say the first thing is to make money, and then we'll see. This is a wrong point of view. All aspects of life are equally important. You cannot postpone life "for later."

THE ENERGY OF MONEY

Internal and external energies create harmony within your life and can make you successful.

There are four kinds of internal energies: Body, Mind,

Soul, and Spirit.

Body—Exercise and good physical health create confidence within you. Those who neglect physical development violate the harmony of body and mind, which is inherent in humankind from childhood. All children, after barely learning to walk, start to move constantly—running, jumping, doing somersaults, climbing trees, etc. In this way, children contribute to the development of their intellects.

The effect of physical training on the activity of the cerebral cortex has long been proven. Any sport exercises, and even the simplest movements, help stimulate the thinking process. This is the reason many people think well when walking. Do not forget to take care of your physical condition, which determines the state of the spiritual.

Mind—Your mind has endless possibilities. By developing your memory, thinking, and intelligence, your mind becomes a tool. When you use this tool properly, it will enable you to realize your wildest dreams.

Remember that your abilities determine your capabilities.

STORY OF BEES

What can bees do and what power do they possess? Bees are able to make honey, build their own home (in this case, among the insects, only bees have architectural abilities), pollinate flowers, utilize an internal GPS system, reproduce, and protect their home. Everyone knows what bees can do when someone invades their territory.

Bees know each other and are able to transmit information to one another. They are able to maintain the required temperature in their homes. It turns out that bees have forty-nine abilities.

Do you know how many cells there are in a bee's brain? Only ten thousand cells. It is a pity that people mostly do not use their abilities as productively as a bee does, although the human brain contains thirty-six billion cells. One scientist has estimated that if scientists put one human brain cell on top of each other, like a high-rise building, they would get a height comparable to fourteen times the distance to the moon and back. You have the ability for amazing things if you simply use your mind. So what you are capable of?

Soul—All parents love their children. They work to earn money so they can provide them with an education. This is the power of love, parental love. The child does not make the parents work; the parents work out of love.

If a man loves a woman, he is willing to risk his own life to protect her. He is ready to do whatever she wants. This is the power of love. When a man loves, he is ready to move mountains. Imagine what you could achieve personally and within your business by applying the same state of mind!

Did you know that in difficult times, in times of change, it is women who quickly adapt, and not men? Women have a maternal instinct. Men often get stuck in their own intellect. While men logically think through the options, women are already acting. Even when men achieve impressive results, they often owe it to the women who inspired them. By simply saying, "My dear, do you think it may be better to do it like this," she encourages him to move forward. She comes up with the idea, and he begins to analyze, to think, *why not?*

PARABLE OF WEALTH, SUCCESS, AND LOVE

A woman, from the comfort of her home, saw three old men with long white beards sitting in front of her porch. She did not know any of them. She said, "I do not know you, but you must be hungry. Please come in and share our lunch."

They responded, "We cannot enter the house all together."

"May I ask why?"

One of the old men explained, pointing to each in turn, "His name is Wealth. His name is Success. My name is Love. Go and talk with your husband and decide which one of us you want to invite."

The woman told her husband all the things she had heard. The man was delighted and exclaimed, "How nice! Let us invite Wealth! Let him come to our house and fill it with affluence."

The wife was not sure she agreed with her husband, "My dear! Why don't we invite Success?"

Their daughter heard the discussion between her mother and father. She exclaimed, "Is it not better to invite Love in? Imagine how wonderful it would be to have our whole house filled with love!"

Listening to their daughter's advice, the husband said to his wife, "Go out and invite Love to be our guest."

The woman went out and asked the three old men, "Which one of you is Love? Please, come in and be our guest."

One of the old men got up and went into the house. Then the other two got up and followed after him.

Surprised, the woman turned to Wealth and Success and asked, "I only invited Love; why did you come, too?"

They replied, "If you had only invited Wealth or Success in, the other two would have left. However, you invited Love in, and wherever Love goes, we follow."

Spirit—Spirit manifests itself in the harmony of the three energies—Body, Mind, and Soul. Some people say, "I am spiritually evolving, improving. Why do I need the money? Material things do not interest me. I'm above it all."

How can you build a house without a foundation? You need to have a foundation. It's the same thing here. How can you develop spiritually if the body is not in order?

Your body has its own needs, and your spiritual attitude depends on your physical condition. Do you remember the old saying, "Healthy body, healthy mind"? Both the mind and the body work together.

The strength of your soul manifests itself when you have thought of everything and are in a successful state of mind. You are determined to win and never give up, despite all the obstacles.

When you earn lots of money, you feel good. You consider yourself a good person. However, it should be noted that goodness and kindness can come from either a state of weakness or a state of strength. People react differently to wealth. Some persons with a lot of money may become arrogant and even address people differently. Sometimes they may even stop talking to people or ignore them altogether, become too self-important and look down on others, or even find faults with family or friends. They become difficult to please and unpleasant to be around. While they may feel they are being kind, their feeling represents a kindness coming from a state of weakness. Wealth will only magnify this response. The more money they accumulate, the more they will lose touch with reality.

This inherent weakness will manifest itself in everything. Having more money will not change you or help you. You will become even weaker with a lot money. If you are prone to drinking, then you will drink more. If you like to shop, you will shop more. If you are passionate about politics, then you will spend more to achieve power.

Money is like a generator. You can use it to light the house or cook food. However, if you don't understand proper safety in using it, you can cause more harm than good.

For example, imagine your child whines, cries, and throws a tantrum, demanding something each time you go shopping. You may indulge your child and give in to stop the crying. Rather than stopping, your child will begin to do this more and more frequently. The more you try to do something, the more it bothers your child. Whatever you do, no matter how hard you try, your child will always be dissatisfied with something. Because the concept of "more" does not change the habits; it also does not affect the character.

You need to realize that in order for money to benefit you and for you to have happiness, kindness should come from a state of strength. You cannot force yourself to be compassionate. Some people are good and kind because they are strong. If they become rich, this inherent goodness will be magnified and they will be even nicer. Many rich people who have achieved something on their own have a very good heart. They dream of someone to support; their dream is to really help someone. They want to have good students who could, in turn, teach the skill. They have the strength of kindness.

Change yourself in the beginning. Make it so that kindness is second nature to you. Then when you do achieve something, this inherent kindness will manifest itself in noble deeds.

LEVELS OF SUCCESS

The only way to learn something is to do something.
~GEORGE BERNARD SHAW

There are five different levels of success, which we will discuss over the next few sections. Please remember these levels as you read through the details in this and the following chapters.

1. Action

2. Technique

3. Acceptance

4. Perception

5. New Vision

LEVEL ONE: ACTION

You agree that you must take some action in life to better yourself. The result of your actions is the success that you have achieved so far. Today's way of life is the result of yesterday's ideas and yesterday's dreams.

If you want to change something in your life, you need to do more now than you did yesterday. Now you may say, "I made a lot of changes, yet everything remains the same!"

That is not true.

Look at the ant: He never lets obstacles stop him. The ant does not give up. The ant keeps looking for a solution until one is found. The ant's persistence, dedication, and hard work are to be envied. For the ant, there are no insurmountable obstacles or unattainable goals.

Some people give up on their dreams while pursuing them because they do not have perseverance or faith. They may be one step away from success, yet their lack of confidence and belief in themselves causes them to quit.

Consider the parable of the elephant.

One boy loved the circus. He liked the colorful, fun, exciting performances. The circus came to his city, and the boy asked his father to go see it. The boy liked the elephant the most and was eager to see it. The elephant worked wonders: lifting weights, juggling, walking on his hind legs. The boy was determined to see an elephant up close. He begged his father to go to the open-air cages where the animals were kept. There the boy saw that the elephant had a chain on one leg. The chain was attached to a peg driven into the ground. It would take hardly any effort for the mighty elephant to pull out the peg and leave.

The boy asked his father, "Dad! Why doesn't the elephant go to be free in the jungle? He can easily pull out the peg and do it. He's so strong!"

His father replied, "Because he is trained and he has

become accustomed to his position."

This was true, but it was also because the elephant was captured when he was very little and chained very securely. Every day, when he was young and lonely, he kept trying to free himself from the chains. He beat his foot on the ground, trying to pull the other foot chain off. He was tired, beaten down, and out of power.

Finally the day came when he recognized his own limitation and became resigned to his fate, knowing that he would never be able to break free. Now, despite the fact that he had grown up and become a great and mighty elephant, he was still convinced that he could not break free.

The elephant remembered that once he could not break free, and, worst of all after that, he gave up. He did not test his strength and capabilities. The majority of people live like the elephant, not believing in themselves, because they tried something once, and it did not work.

LEVEL TWO: TECHNIQUE

Technique is the choice of direction, or specialization. You need to know your direction in life so as to not waste a lot of time. People finishing school tend to choose a profession. Some will become engineers, some teachers, some lawyers . . . that is the technique. Your specialty is what you have chosen to pursue. For example, in the field of entrepreneurship, technique is the industry that you choose. Choose the industry you are most passionate about.

LEVEL THREE: ACCEPTANCE

Many people only reach the third level. For example, you say to yourself, "Yes, I'm a good worker, a good person. I deserve respect and recognition. My children love me. My parents, relatives, and friends say only good things about me.

My colleagues respect me." That's how we reassure ourselves.

We all are living in the first three levels, but it is at this third level that many stop. They do not try to climb to the fourth level because it is no longer their dream. The average person thinks, *I built a career and gained recognition. I have money, a job, a good family, and the children are fed, clothed, and have shoes. So everything is good and I am happy.* This a statement of contentment, a justification for doing just enough. It may all be true, but what if you could do much more?

In this case, people no longer climb up the ladder of life, and they are content with an average level of income. People come to me and say, "I have twenty years of experience." I reply, "No, you have one year of work experience that you repeated twenty times." This is because only one year is spent on the accumulation of experience; afterwards is just mere repetition.

When you think of life this way, you can see how a slight shift in your thinking can create major results. When persons are comfortable, they forget about their original goals and are not inspired to go any further.

However, there is a higher level. In level four, nothing changes . . . this is an intermediate level. Only on the fifth level do things change in a very remarkable way. Do not stop halfway! Boldly go for the top and strive for your dreams.

LEVEL FOUR: PERCEPTION

Although I mentioned that level four is an intermediate level, in reality, it is extremely important. Bodo Shafer calls it "glasses," referring to the level of human perception.

"Glasses" means looking at the world with your own eyes, having your own point of view, and being able to distinguish important things amidst various minor distractions. We are often so focused on nonsense and unimportant details when we look through our "glasses" that we sometimes fail to see the truth.

We need to live right. If persons have "bad glasses," they do not even recognize wealth and do not understand it. We need the "correct glasses" that will help us appreciate the meaning of wealth.

It is better to be rich. You can help feed the poor, help the weary traveler, and help the elderly. You can help educate a gifted student who is unable to afford an education. You can help treat sick children. In the world, three billion people live on $1 a day. There are two billion people who cannot read and write. One billion are undernourished.

Unlike them, we live very well. Remember to keep in mind that in difficult times, someone supported us, too. Therefore, we must help support those around us. There are a lot of needy people in the world, even among our friends. You can say, "My help will not change anything; there are too many, and I cannot help everyone."

In response, I will tell you a parable.

Once a vacationer was walking along the beach. The sea, the wind, the wet sand, the setting sun . . . how beautiful! Suddenly, in the distance, he saw a man. The man bent down, took something in his hands, and then threw it into the water. When the man came closer, the vacationer saw that the man had picked up a starfish that washed up on shore and was returning it to the sea. He was surprised and said, "Good evening! Can you tell me what you are doing?"

"I returned the starfish to its home. The tide is so weak that all the starfish were on the beach. If they do not get thrown back into the sea, they will all die."

"I understand," the vacationer replied, "but there are a thousand starfish on the beach. You cannot throw all of them back; there are too many of them! And the same thing is happening on hundreds of beaches all along the coast. Do you realize that nothing will change and that what you are doing doesn't matter?"

The man smiled, bent down, picked up another starfish, threw it into the water, and said, "It mattered to that one."

I once asked a guy how much he earned. He said, "$300." I asked, "And why not $3,000?" He thought about it, then said that so far, no one had asked him about it, no one had spoken to him on the subject. It was as if he expected someone to tell him about his abilities, that he was able to earn more, and instill self-confidence in him.

Now ask yourself the same question—why you are earning what you earn and no more? Record your answer in two sentences.

_____

_____

_____

_____

_____

When I was asked this question, I made excuses. Excuse after excuse came out. They were all true; however, I avoided the real truth. I accused my country, its citizens, and the factory where I worked. It was the truth, but the real truth is what I avoided. It was a question about what I wanted from life. These are the "glasses."

Excuses can always be found. Do you like being in a position where you have to constantly make excuses? After all, there is no excuse that will replace the result. Is it not better to change everything to achieve your goals and realize your dreams? Sometimes the solution is not where we think it is. External circumstances are deceptive. Because of our routines, monotonous everyday life, we fail to see the most important things.

Think about it, because if you become rich, you can buy paintings created by the best artists. You can listen to any music, buy cars, homes, and all the appliances you have ever dreamed about. You can go out to shop and not have to think about the price. This is financial freedom. We all deserve more, and we can achieve this.

The fourth level is about finding the "right glasses." This level is complex and unique. To start, you have to become an observer—you become a student. Sometimes it's easier to become a teacher than a pupil.

Consider the following story.

The student went to the master and said, "I want to learn the secrets of life, and I can learn them from you."

The teacher asked him to talk about himself. The student told the master where he studied, what progress he had achieved, and what kind of experience he had acquired. He gave several examples. Then, when the teacher began giving him lessons, the student said, "Teacher, maybe if we do it this way, it would be better!"

In another lesson, the student said, "Why not try it a different way?" Then he asked in the next lesson, "May we do it differently?"

And then the teacher said, "You see, the fact of the matter is, it is easy to become the teacher, but it is hard to be a student."

"Glasses": this is that student, who is able in every situation to see something good, to learn and grow in all directions, in all spheres of life.

Bodo Shafer has a story about the American speaker Stephen Covey.

Covey traveled all over the country doing presentations for large audiences. Once Covey rode the train to another city. At one of the stops, a man with three children boarded the train. The man sat down and began to look out the window, as if enjoying the passing scenery.

The three children did not behave very well. They began running around the car, shouting and disturbing the other passengers. In the end, one of the children ran up to Covey and hit him in the legs.

He quietly got up, went to their father, and politely said, "Sir, do you see that your children aren't giving anyone in the car a chance to rest? Could you please tell your children to settle down and act properly?" Then he quietly returned to his seat, satisfied that his request was made tactfully and with dignity.

Events began to move unexpectedly. The father looked out the window for some time as if nothing had happened. After a few minutes, he turned to Covey, looked at him, and said, "I'm sorry that my children disturbed you and caused you or anyone else any trouble. We have just come from the hospital where their mother had passed away. I do not know what to do. Maybe this is the way they're coping with it."

How do you think Covey felt after hearing this? He wrote that it was a very powerful lesson that life had given him, one that he would never forget.

We need the correct glasses to see through all the obstacles on the way to achieving our goals and dreams. Sometimes the answers can be found where you do not or least expect to find them.

If you have visited the fourth level, you need to get ready for the fifth. It is here, on the fifth level, that changes occur. You will receive a new vision for yourself. How does the new vision of yourself look? Think about this question and try to understand its meaning.

LEVEL FIVE: NEW VISION

We live in a world where everyone has a dream. Deep

down, everyone dreams to achieve something, to do good. Look around: everything in this plan is the same, but there is something special that makes us different. That is how much we believe in our dreams and in our ability to see ourselves from the outside.

Imagine two people who have similar goals. One achieves what he or she desires, and the second one does not. Why? Are they not both worthy, do they not each have a dream? Of course! So what makes us all different? It is our inner attitude that makes us unique. If you can see yourself from the outside, you really can change your life and realize your dreams. You will have a special feeling inside yourself.

Look at a successful woman. How she speaks. How she talks on the phone. How she walks. Her behavior reflects her inner spirit. After all, how do optimists think? If they arrive late for their train, they believe that they arrived early for the next train. Successful people have a special gift. It is the ability to feel yourself in a special role. Imagine yourself successful and believe like a winner.

PARABLE OF "YOUR OWN OPINION"

A young man arrived at an oasis while traveling through the desert. He had a drink of water and asked an old man resting next to the spring, "What kind of people live here?"

The old man, in turn, asked the young man, "What kind of people live there, where you come from?"

"A bunch of selfish people with bad intentions," replied the young man.

"You will you find the same kind of people here," said the old man.

That same day, another young man arrived at the oasis to quench his thirst while traveling. Seeing the old man, he greeted him and asked, "What kind of people live in this place?"

The old man asked, in response, the same question, "What kind of people live there, where you come from?"

"Lovely! Honest, hospitable, and friendly. It was painful to part with them," the young man replied.

"You will find the same kind of people here," said the old man.

A third man, who had heard the replies to both of the young men's questions, asked the old man, "How could you give two such different answers to the same question?"

The old man replied, "Each of us can see only what we carry in our heart. Those who do not find anything good at home cannot find anything else, neither here nor in any other place."

If we do not like something in the world around us, then what makes us most upset are not the things that are around us, but rather our opinion about them. That is why you need to change yourself before you start this journey. Make it so that you have kindness from strength. Then, when you do achieve something, it will manifest itself in noble deeds.

SYMBOL OF WEALTH

Have you ever noticed that each religion has its own symbols? That each country has its own flag and coat of arms? Their own type of currency? Why do you think they have them? What purpose do they serve?

Symbols give strength! If you have some things in your house that belonged to your ancestors, they will be priceless to you. They remind you of the connection between the generations. They are a symbol of the past.

Wealth also has its own symbol. If you walk into any commercial company, you will immediately see the company's sign on the front of the building. On the walls of the office will be the company logo, symbolizing the scope of its activities and progress. You will start to believe in this company. Symbols of wealth, likewise, give us both strength and confidence.

That is why symbols are very important for us. You need to think of your own symbol and determine its design. This symbol should be where you sleep and work, and it should accompany you everywhere. When you are going through difficulties, when you feel despair or are simply tired, look at the symbol of wealth. You will see that it fills you with energy and strength. And this feeling is inexplicable.

What is your symbol of wealth? Do you have something in your life or your family that is a symbol of your family or your success? Think about your success, your job, and your family. What would your symbol of wealth look like?

_____

_____

_____

_____

_____

MONEY LESSON

Let's try another exercise. Carry all the cash that you have now and keep it with you wherever you go. The amount will vary with each person. You may have $200, $500, or even $1,000. You have to get used to constantly having the money with you, without fear that it can be stolen, that you will spend it, or that you will just lose it.

First, it will give you confidence. Second, you will learn how to accurately handle money and restrain yourself in certain situations when you are tempted to spend the money. Without these qualities, we cannot even talk about managing large sums of money.

I learned all this the hard way. My experience on the streets made managing money extremely difficult. Then I needed to sleep in railway stations, to go hungry, and to spend all my money on training.

Do you remember when I told about my first visit to Moscow? I spent all my money and had no way to go home. Did I travel there with the intention of doing heavy physical labor? No. I always had a dream to study in Moscow.

Many people think, *I will work temporarily and set the dream aside.* After working tirelessly, I had the revelation and understood then why people often remain poor. They have worthy goals, but their job or immediate need for money moves them in the completely opposite direction.

We do not realize one important thing. In order to succeed, you need to work hard, and not necessarily at easy tasks. Sometimes it is simpler and easier just to go with the flow. But doing that does nothing to help you achieve your goals. You quickly find yourself at the bottom.

If what you are doing does not bring you closer to your dream, then why are you doing it? You will soon forget about your original purpose, and gradually it will become an unattainable mirage. That is what I finally understood.

Many people dream about one thing but do something else. Eventually you will be at the beginning again. If what you are doing at the present time does not lead you to wealth, that means you have made your own choice. And it is to be poor—this is your fate.

Then another thought came to me. *Do you think if you work with your hands and feet, it is possible to become rich? Do you know at least one person who works doing heavy physical labor, who has become rich? No, not even one.*

I promised myself in that moment that I would never do that type of work. I realized that I have a choice: either I am doing physical labor, or I am working with my mind.

The Lord will never leave us, believe me. When I was desperate, sitting on the park bench in Moscow, soaking wet and not knowing what to do, I prayed and asked God for wisdom and understanding. Unconsciously, I removed my shoes to shake out what got into them. Suddenly, I saw in the bottom of my shoes two 500-ruble bills.

At first I did not believe it! I thought they looked like advertising stickers. I took the bills in my hands, held them, and they were real. It was at this moment that I firmly promised myself that I would change everything. That this money would be the beginning of my wealth.

As soon as I made the decision, my life changed like a fairy tale. I believed in it. Immediately after finding the money on the soles of my shoes, I promised myself that I would learn to manage money.

As Bodo Schafer says, "We need to learn to manage money before it will appear, and when it appears, it will be easier."

While sitting on the park bench, it became clear to me that the world has everything in abundance. God has given us so many natural resources to use. They are on the ground, under the ground, in the water, and under the water. However, we do not appreciate them.

I realized that I did not have the same inner state that I had before. Something had changed inside of me. Before visiting Moscow, my self-perception was that I had grown up in a wealthy family. I had always been well-dressed and had money.

This mind-set lasted until the restructuring of the former Soviet Union and the war that followed. After that, I stopped taking care of myself. I did not pay any attention to my clothing, and for a long time I did not buy expensive things, even though at times I had the money. I had no feeling of my own worth. When I looked in the mirror, I did not look like myself. I had dirty clothes, dirty shoes, and no purpose in life.

Suddenly, I realized that I constantly had the fear of losing my money. My body literally soaked up the habit of living in poverty. This happened unconsciously; however, if I went on like this, I knew the habits would stay with me. I did not want that to happen and said firmly to myself, "I will allow myself to be rich. I will live very rich." After I made this decision, something unusual happened, and I started making good money.

I started with one hundred rubles. Two weeks later, I began to earn three hundred, five hundred, one thousand rubles per day. The food normally cost twenty rubles. For three hundred rubles, you could eat in a very nice restaurant. You know what I did? I did not touch the one thousand rubles that I had found in the park, and I spent the rest of my money. I set a goal to spend all the money I had. I went to the most expensive restaurants, ordered the most exquisite meals, and bought the most fashionable clothes so that I could feel like a rich man. I had the thought that I would rather spend the money than have someone else take it away.

At that time, I came to realize something very important: how you treat yourself is how others will treat you. If you do not respect yourself, then other people will treat you the same way . . . with no respect. That is why I felt it was necessary to go to expensive restaurants, dress nicely, etc.

I also did one more thing. I approached a taxi driver and asked how much it would cost for an hour's drive. He said that it depended on where I wanted to go. I answered that I had nowhere in mind; I just want to go for a ride.

The taxi driver asked, "Why do you want a taxi and don't know where you want to go?"

I replied, "You know, I always had a dream to ride around the streets of Moscow and see it."

He drove me around Moscow every day. And he was making good money every day. Why did I do that? To feel rich, to be more confident. When a persons feels and act confidently, everything they do leads to success.

After a while, I began to feel like a rich man. I began to earn 1,500 to 2,000 rubles a day. In those years, that was around $400 to $500. In my home country, it was possible to buy an apartment for that amount.

For the same reason, I went to the train station and found those who had recently arrived in Moscow who had not yet found a job. It was not important where they came from or what nationality they were. I fed all of them at my own expense. Sometimes, I would take care of as many as fifty to one hundred people at a time. They were very grateful to have the help.

The most interesting thing is that I started to feel rich. Do you know how good it feels when you are able to help someone else?

Mahatma Gandhi said, "What you get allows you to survive, and what you give helps you to live." These are words I will remember for a lifetime. For two weeks, I continued to walk to the station and to feed these people every day.

You know, not long ago, I was earning one hundred rubles a day and spent twenty rubles on food. Now I was renting the most expensive apartment. It was very comfortable and cozy. If you are not afraid, and allow yourself to feel like a rich man, a new life full of prosperity and success comes to you.

You need to allow yourself to feel wealthy.

There, on the park bench, I hated my style of life. I hated policemen for taking away my money. I was hurting inside and was offended. Now, I am so grateful to them. If it was not for them, I would not be who I am today. Then, I was angry at them. Today, I feel like a very different person.

When I am in Moscow, I try to go to the park. I will find the familiar bench where my life changed and just sit. That gives me strength and helps me to go forward. Most people seem to understand when I am talking about myself; however, not all people let themselves believe it. Some people can convince themselves that everything they do will lead to success, and it will. If some people convince themselves every day that something will not work, then it won't. In either case, the persons making the choices are correct.

For myself, the main thing I understood was that there are two types of people: (1) Those who work with their hands and count the money in their head. They need so much for rent, to pay utilities, and to pay their bills. (2) Those who earn with their heads and then use their hands to count the money.

This realization changed my life forever.

In two months, after making the decision to change my life, I became the manager of the Kiev Market. In six months, I bought a two-bedroom apartment in an affluent neighborhood. A year later, I owned my house in Moscow. Some can work all their lives in Moscow, but can never buy a place to live in. I did it in six months. And in your life, there will come a time when you will earn more in one day than you did in a year. This will only happen if you make a firm decision and do not quit when things get difficult.

Where there is no will, there is no way.
~GEORGE BERNARD SHAW

The Lord will never leave a person.

One day, a man was walking through the desert. He was very tired, because his journey lasted for many days, and he was thirsty. When the traveler's strength was running out, he began to pray.

"Lord, I'm dying of thirst. In the Bible, you promised that you would help us, that you will always be with us; even in the most difficult moments, you will support us. I have traveled for many days, and I have no strength left. Behind me are only traces of my feet; you were not with me; I'm alone."

After praying, in tears of fatigue and exhaustion, he fell asleep. Then he dreamed of two reflections in the sky.

He said, "Lord, what is it?"

The Lord said to him, "When you saw only one set of footprints in the sand—those are my footprints. I was carrying you."

MONEY MUSCLES

Do you feel that you are slowly gaining confidence? You need to constantly have faith in yourself.

When you walk into a store, you look around. All of a sudden, you see something that is on sale. This is the lowest price you have ever seen for this item, and you really want to buy it. Even if you were not planning to purchase it because you already have the same thing at home, you still want to buy it. If the clerk wants to help you with the selection, you can politely refuse by saying, "I'm just looking. Thank you." However, you know that you can buy this item if you wanted to.

Having money readily available inspires confidence. This is especially noticeable in women. Watch women in any store. At a glance, you will be able to determine each one's level of income. If some members from the family visit who are wealthier than the others, they tend to say more than the others. This happens because they are more self-confident.

Therefore, when you carry money, you train your money muscles. It is like a singer rehearsing who prepares for months, but then sings only once. Making a music album sometimes takes years.

Do not be afraid that your money can be lost or stolen. Your money you will teach you discipline.

Researchers in the United States conducted a unique experiment. They photographed five hundred people. All of them were asked what they were afraid of. Some said they were afraid of being robbed, while others said they were afraid of being killed. All their answers were recorded.

The photos were then taken to a prison. The researchers showed inmates convicted of robbery and murder the pictures. They were asked whom they would choose to be their victims.

The experiment showed that robbers often picked those who feared robberies. The murderers accurately chose the people who were afraid of being killed. At the same time, the criminals could not explain their choices. So try to overcome your fears. Remember, a negative psychological state attracts trouble and provokes criminals.

It is very important to deal with your fears. You need to train yourself to confidently carry large sums of money with you.

At one of my training sessions, after the topic of money muscles, a woman said that she was not afraid to carry a lot of money. She had twenty-five years of experience as a cashier and always carried a significant amount of money with her.

I told her, "Well, let me give you twenty thousand dollars. Then you will have to walk around with the money all day and return it tomorrow."

She agreed. I gave her the money. She hid the money in her bag and left.

After that, I gave the other students the task to follow her. They were to follow her wherever she went and record her on video. The videos showed that when subjects rode on the bus, they concentrated on her bag. Her face was very tense and serious. It was noticeable that the woman was stressed out and very worried.

When she got off the bus, she walked to her apartment building. She saw that there was a group of strangers by the entrance to her building. These, too, were my students. They just stood and talked, watching her. The woman decided not to go past them to get to her apartment. She walked around the building. She had already walked around the building twice when the students called me and explained the situation. I asked them to move away from the entrance.

Once they left, the woman quickly ran into her apartment. The next day, when she came to school, she handed over the money. We all watched the videos together. When she saw herself on the videos, she admitted that was not easy to carry large sums of money without worrying about them.

All people like cash; however, they are afraid to take responsibility for large sums. The fear of losing the money impedes confidence in such cases.

When I tell the students at training that is necessary for them to put their capabilities above the money, all the participants understand and agree with it. When it comes to real money, however, not all of them can overcome their concerns and fears.

I once conducted an experiment with several groups of students in different cities. During the training, I asked all the students to bring all the cash they had at home with them the next day. I told them the money was needed for a training game. All of the students brought their money. The amounts varied depending on each participant's financial situation. The money was carefully counted, and serial numbers on the currency were recorded. The amount each person contributed was also recorded. When this was completed, the person in charge gave me all the money. To conclude the training, I announced that all the money would stay with me and that I would keep it until the following year. Exactly one year later, all the money would be returned. I explained that this was being done to ensure that the trainees practiced and were able to understand one of the basic rules of successful people: put your capabilities higher than the money; then the money will come to you and will serve you.

Theoretically, all the participants of the training

understood what I was doing. They accepted it and were okay with it. In practice, this is very difficult to do. Their doubts, fears, and lack of confidence interfered with their abilities. They all reacted to my announcement differently. Some of the students were frowning. Some of them were smiling. Others were calm and thinking about something else.

From the four groups upon which I conducted the experiment, only two of the groups made it through the experiment and overcame their fears. At the same time, in St. Petersburg, a girl was in the office crying. She explained that her car had been stolen. Her parents sent her money to buy a new car, and that was the money she had brought for the experiment. When I asked her to calm down and take her money, she tearfully refused. It was evident that she was struggling with herself. She, of course, still wanted to get her money back. She had already realized the principles of successful people and did not want to show weakness. She did not take the money. It was a small victory for her. It is exactly people like this young woman who achieve their goals and become wealthy.

Members of another group persistently asked me whether or not the money would remain in my custody until the next year. I replied, "Yes, I am not joking," and that this was indeed the case. Especially since I was leaving the next day. After class, all the group members left, but it was evident that their doubts and fears would not let them rest.

I left all the money collected with the leader of the group. I requested that the money be returned the following day. The next morning, I arrived at the station. To my surprise, nearly the entire group was waiting for me there. Apparently, they were not able to overcome their fears. I explained that all the money was with the group leader and that he was instructed to return their money to them. They all then realized their mistake.

They were not able to overcome their doubts; the doubts

were stronger than they were. The students who were able to overcome their doubts met with me a year later. They thanked me for a useful lesson.

Indecision is worse than failure. It is better to try, and make mistakes, than to do nothing. Mistakes leave us with experience and knowledge; our indecision leaves fear and doubts. A true understanding of the rule gives a person strength and self-confidence; it also points the way to success. If you cannot have a calm and confident attitude toward money, whether it is a big or small amount, you can never become rich. If you are afraid of small amounts of money, you will never have large amounts. That is why you need to try to become a master over money. Put your opportunities and your profession above the money. Only then can you become a successful and independent person.

Do you know who may be called an independent person? One who can fulfill all that he had promised himself, his wife, his children, and friends. If you promised to make your wife's life a fairy tale, then do it. If you promised to develop your friend's talents, then develop them. If you promised that you would find a way to get along with your wife's relatives, then, even though it may be difficult, find it. If you promised to give your children a good education, then do it. This is true freedom and independence. I believe we all deserve it.

People may ask you, "Well, why do you carry around that much money?" You can respond that you are training your money muscles. Then continue to do so, even if people think that you are weird. It is better to be strange, but rich, successful, and happy, than to be a very reasonable, but poor, loser.

I once flew from the airport in Moscow. I had forty-some-odd thousand dollars in cash on me. It was a pretty decent amount. The money was in a pocket inside my jacket, which I took off and put on top of my luggage. We still had some time before the flight left. I decided to go to the bathroom before the flight boarded. Starting towards the bathroom, I suddenly said to myself, "I have around forty thousand dollars in my jacket pocket." Although I had asked a woman standing near my luggage to keep an eye on my things, all the same, I wanted to go back to get the money and take it with me. I was thinking about what could happen to the money in my absence!

I really wanted to go back, but I stopped myself and said, "Either you go quietly about your business, without thinking or worrying about the money, because you have big plans. Or go back and get the money that you are worried about, and you will be satisfied with this amount."

I willed myself to continue forward, although my legs trembled. I told myself that I did not want to stay at the level of the amount of money I had. *I have a big dream,* I thought to myself. *I will not have to worry and stress about that money.*

With each step, I had more and more doubts. What if the jacket fell and all the money fell out on the floor? What if someone touched my things and noticed the money? Thousands of these thoughts whirled in my head.

Even in the bathroom, my concerns continued. I thought, *Maybe I should get up and go and see if everything is okay with the money. Then, I can come back and continue.* So I *was* afraid to lose this amount. It seems funny to me now, but then, it was all very serious. Still, I managed to overcome my fears.

Fears hold us back. They interfere with you realizing your dream. Fear takes away your confidence, and forces you to accept dismal results. Do not give in to your fears. Believe in your dream. And remember that if someone asks to borrow money, you can lend it, but only lend 10 percent of the amount they request.

NOTES

CHAPTER 5

HOW TO SAVE

Money is plentiful for those who understand
the simple laws which govern its acquisition.
~ GEORGE S. CLASON

This is how I was taught to manage money. I will try to teach you. First, consider the distribution of your income by using this model.

BUDGET MODEL

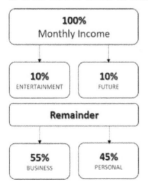

When you learn how to manage money, it will come on its own to you. Money comes to those who know how to work with it and what to do with it.

If you do not know what to do with money, it is better not to do anything. First, find out what, where, and how to learn to manage money.

Then do it later.

Let's say that your monthly income is not a stable salary. The amount that you earn from your labor, your abilities, and your knowledge can fluctuate in one direction or another, depending on the state of your affairs. You spend money on rent, insurance, education, clothes, food, etc. (For entertainment and leisure, as always, there is not enough money.)

What is left from your monthly income? It is like a never-ending financial swamp. We all go through the same thing. People say, "If I make more money, then there will be something left to save. That's when I'll start saving." When you start earning more, you will want more and spend more. And nothing will change.

About six thousand years ago, Babylon was the richest city in the world. It became so thanks to one man, who created the "House of Knowledge." Once he was asked, "Everybody wants to be rich; everyone has a chance and equal opportunities. But then why do some people become rich while the majority languishes in poverty? What is the difference between them?"

The man replied, "The rich know what we call necessary expenses."

He had the following in mind.

Assume that your income steadily increased: in the last month, you earned $1,000 and lived on that amount. This month you earned $1,500, and you have spent it all. Next month's income rises to $2,000, and your needs will rise up to this amount. Even if you earn $3,000, the cost will correspond to a new income level.

SCHEDULE OF INCOME AND EXPENSES

At $1,500, you lived pretty well. Why does this happen? That's because the appetites are growing and you have new requirements. Never concentrate on consumer spending. An Indian sage said, "The temptations of this world are like saltwater: the more a person drinks it, the more they thirst." When you buy vegetables, fruit, food, clothing, etc., you increase the income of the people who grew the crops or made the things that you purchased. Because, at any rate, your expenditures are someone's income.

Why do people spend more when they start earning more? They consume with the hope that next month they will earn even more. However, they have not even thought about how to do this. Why does their income not increase? Because the level of the individuals does not meet the higher level of income. Income does not raise the individuals. These people are not knowledgeable about money management. They do not possess the ability and skills of how to earn a lot of money and how to save money. So remember to pay yourself first before you pay the rest of the world.

Why are even so-called rich people not confident in the future? They travel in expensive cars and go to expensive restaurants, but they nevertheless have gloomy and sad faces. They wear very expensive clothing, but they know that if there are two or three months of a business recession, they cannot repay the credit for their expenditures. If the recession lasts a year, money will be very tight. It makes them very anxious. All this is because they did not pay themselves first. Successful, wealthy people do it differently. First, they set aside a certain amount, then spend what remains.

That is why we have created a model. It helps you to achieve your goals. In the model, you are the owner and the employee.

From the total amount that you earn, you need to set aside 10 percent for your future. This is not your money. It is money for your dreams. You have no right to touch it. Another 10 percent is put toward leisure and entertainment. If you need to go somewhere, look at the expense of the entertainment. If you need to buy someone a gift, take a look at its expense. You need to have a system. Once you create a system, it will begin to work independently. Then money will come to you and will become an integral part of the system. You will be surprised at how quickly it increases your well-being.

Let us return to our calculations. Now the remaining amount will be considered as 100 percent. From this sum, we will allocate 55 percent to the business account. The remaining 45 percent is placed in your own account. Sometimes it happens that you have increased your income 1.5 times, then fall back below the previous level. Why? You just could not handle the responsibility.

For example, let's say your income is $1,000. Ten percent of that amount is $100—this is for your future. Another 10 percent is $100—for leisure and entertainment. The remaining amount is $800, divided by the business account (55 percent = $440), and your personal account (45 percent = $360). Even if this amount is not enough to go to a restaurant or sit in a cafe, still save only 10 percent, no more.

Money will come to someone who knows what to do with it. It is necessary not only to acquire these skill, but also to learn how to apply them. If your four types of internal energies are not in harmony, the money will elude you, no matter how smart you are. Therefore, your internal energies must all match.

Remember the first rule—the income does not increase the level of development of the individual, but the level of development of the individual will increases the income. When persons are not responsible for their own future, their incomes decrease. It turns out that no matter how much you earn, your income equals your expenses. The model account that I showed you will help you to break this vicious cycle. The effect will be that you are essentially an employee and that you own fixed salary from your income. Then your costs will not grow as before.

This means that if you earn more the next month, the higher amount is set aside on the company's account. And 45 percent is always placed in your own account. There may be days that you are out of work, and this money will be very helpful.

Why do this? So you do not increase your level of spending. Suppose your income increases; the costs should be kept at the same level. How do you determine the amount of your salary today? Write today's date and last year's date. Then start counting from last year's date to the present date.

Calculate how much you have earned during this year. From this amount, subtract exactly 45 percent. Divide the amount by twelve months. Does this figure please you? No? It does not matter; you still need to follow the set rules. The figure that came out is your fixed monthly salary. You do not have the right to spend any more than that if you really want to become rich. It does not matter how small the amount is or if you do not like it; you still must follow the model.

YOUR CHOICE

You have a choice that you need to make on the basis of information you have received.

1. Make a decision to change your life and start saving money, using the model.
OR

2. Leave everything as it was before, without changing anything.

Either way, you still have to make a decision. There is no other way. To some people, it may seem that the original purpose is not so great. The figures are not as pleasing as you would like. However, from this seed an enormous tree may grow. Anyone can count the number of seeds in an apple. No one can say how many apples can grow from these seeds. This is the first seed.

You will be able to live very nicely, with dignity and self-respect. If you start saving a little now, of course, it will look like a small amount. However, if you do not save anything at all, you will live as indicated by the second arrow.

No one knows what his strength is until he has to use it.
~GOETHE

QUALITY OF LIFE

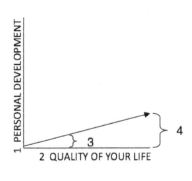

If you start saving, even only slightly, it will look as shown by number 3. After some time, the result will be consistent with number 4. This is a good indicator of your personal development. You will achieve absolutely nothing if you do nothing. That's the difference. Even a slight amount saved changes the situation.

Bodo Schafer said as much in Singapore. After the seminar, one person came up to him and said, "You know, I like what you said. This is correct, but I cannot afford to save money. I am hardly earning enough to live on." Then he reached in and pulled out a cigarette!

Bodo Schafer looked at him and asked, "Are you smoking?!"

"Well, yes, I enjoy smoking," said the man.

Schafer took the calculator and figured how much money the student could save if he did not smoke from age eighteen to sixty. It turned out to be $43,000. On average, most people believed it is only $2. The response he heard was, "I'd rather be smoking."

Schafer added that he had not included any of the interest that could be earned on the money.

"What? I could earn interest on that, too?!" the man exclaimed in surprise.

Schafer explained that the amount of money being saved each year would earn interest and that each year the amount of interest would increase.

The largest percentages obtained are in the last five years.

After all, even Jesus said in Matthew 20:16, "The last shall be first and the first shall be last." How much do you think the man at the seminar would have if he had set aside the money at 14 percent per annum? About 4.5 million dollars and some change.

If you saved $1 each day at 8 percent interest, in thirty years it will be about $1.8 to 2 million dollars. People usually spend more than a dollar a day. Even a small amount saved can change your situation. It may seem to you that this is impossible. You want to put $10,000 into the bank immediately. Why go to the bank for only $100 or even $500? You can keep that at home.

Even a small amount of money can change the situation. Bodo Schafer said that if you are not satisfied with 45 percent, then when you earn more, the 45 percent will also be larger. Would you agree, for example, that 45 percent of $500 is a small amount ($225)? Now, 45 percent of $5,000 is pretty decent money ($2,250). Therefore, do what Jesus did. He said: "Do twice as much!"

I vowed to do more and decided that I would be saving for three years, and I wrote down a specific amount. It was small. However, I put up with it.

You need to accept and adopt this rule, just as I did. No matter how small the initial accumulated amount is. If there is any money left over from the 45 percent, you need to increase the amount to be placed into the future account, up to 15 percent, and then up to 20 percent, 25 percent, 30 percent, 40 percent, even 50 percent. The entertainment account stays at 10 percent no matter what . . . never increase this percentage, even if you earn more.

For example, 10 percent of $10,000 will be a substantial sum ($1,000). Enjoy your life today, because you never know what tomorrow will bring. Enjoy spending the money; however, do not go overboard. Live with dignity, because when you start to earn more, you will have different people around you who have a higher level of income. You will need to dress differently to go to prestigious places. The cost will increase, so you must be prepared for this. Therefore, 10 percent is for entertainment; even if revenues increase, this is normal. We live for today, and then live with dignity, sometimes treating ourselves and the people close to us. Do not forget to save 55 percent in the business account on a consistent basis. Try to calculate on your own how much you will save, even if you are saving small amounts.

DEBTS

If you have any debts, the model changes. It is necessary to change the model. Each month save 10 percent for your future and 20 percent in order to pay debts. The remaining amount we divide by the same percentages into the two accounts. For now, the entertainment account will not exist. Who can have fun when you're in debt? Have you noticed that there are some people who are heavily in debt and still plan a vacation to rest somewhere? People often have a self-defeating habit. Even if they are in debt, they need to be distracted from their problems with the help of entertainment.

Here's a good rule—do not buy and do not take things from the person who has debts. It is written in the Holy Book (Proverbs 22:26–27): "Be not one of those who give pledges, who put up security for debts. If you have nothing with which to pay, why should your bed be taken from under you?"

What is your strategy for managing debt? If you have borrowed money from a relative and think, *If I pay them off quickly, it will be better*, you try to do it quickly. Once you get paid, you pay off the debt. However, if you have no money left because you paid the debt back quickly, you need to borrow money from someone else until you get paid again. What's the difference?!

Therefore, we must set aside only 20 percent on the debt. If creditors are unhappy, then you say, "If you don't want to accept a partial payment, you can be patient and wait until I save the entire amount needed to pay you off."

No matter how long it takes you to pay off your debt, always save 10 percent for your future. This will help you feel confident and secure. Remember that even the slightest amount saved changes the situation.

This is an important thing to understand in your quest to pay off debt. Pay yourself first. This will help you create a future for yourself. There will always be debt. Pay yourself first and also pay the debt. But pay it slowly and not all at once.

If you train yourself to act according to this model, you will develop a pattern of behavior and thinking. For example, as soon as you pay off the debts, your mind will automatically remember certain rules. You will no longer be saving 10 percent; instead, you will be saving 30 percent for your future. From this moment, your savings will grow three times faster.

It turns out that being in debt can be useful. It may cause you to hit rock bottom. It may cause you to want to make a change. If you had not been in debt, you may not have known you needed to change. At one time, debt became a necessary experience for you, and you have learned from it. According to the model, you need to establish a set system. It does not matter how much money you have; the main thing is the system.

What is your system for success?

If you say, "I have very little money. When I have more, then I will do everything in the system," it means that you do not believe in yourself. Have a system and follow it.

If you do not believe in your future, then why live? If you do not believe that you can improve the quality of your life, then why do you continue to study? If you do not believe in your country, your president, your wife (or husband)—that you will be happy with her (him)—do you think this is life? Why deceive yourself? Why save money if you do not believe that tomorrow you will be rich!?

Many people say, "We save money for a rainy day." We were taught, and our relatives told us, to save money during the good times to get us through the bad times. Our minds were trained that money helps us in difficult times.

This is not true. We need to believe in a good future. Therefore, by saving money we create a way of life which we think about and dream about. Sooner or later, every person starts doing so.

Imagine yourself as a bird. Call one wing "Hope" and the other one "Fear." Either you will fly because you want to experience the feeling of free flight, or life will push you and you then will fly from fear. You will not get any enjoyment from the latter.

Notes

_____

_____

_____

_____

_____

_____

_____

_____

_____

_____

_____

_____

_____

_____

_____

_____

_____

_____

_____

_____

_____

_____

_____

_____

_____

_____

_____

_____

_____

CHAPTER 6

HOW TO INVEST

I hear and I forget. I see and I remember.
I do and I understand.
~ CONFUCIUS

There are three levels of investment.

1. Financial protection.

2. Financial security.

3. Financial freedom.

Many people wonder where and why to invest. When you learn how to manage money, it will come on its own in large amounts. Then it will be useful to have knowledge about capital investment. Most people do not know what to do with the extra money, where to invest it, and how to evaluate real-world possibilities. So they carelessly spend it on all sorts of items and experiences they don't necessarily need. Later they start thinking that it would have been possible to invest their money in business and make a profit. But it is too late. The money was already spent.

Remember the parable of the goose that lays golden eggs?

A farmer saw that his goose had laid a golden egg. He did not believe it! He took the egg in his hands and examined it. It was really gold! He went to the jeweler, showed him the egg, and the jeweler paid him. On the second day, the same thing happened—the goose laid another golden egg. It was not too long before the farmer lost his patience. How was the goose doing this? He decided to kill the goose to see how she did it. He slaughtered the goose, but all he found in it was another golden egg.

In other words, the golden egg is the interest or income you get from money you invest. You need to create your own goose that will lay golden eggs. When you have accumulated some money, which means that it is possible to create the goose, it is spent buying new clothes, electronics, jewelry, or a new car, which are not always necessary at the moment. Maybe you want to relax and travel somewhere abroad, although you could vacation somewhere closer. You think that if you buy a car, an apartment, and a lot of gold jewelry, you are already rich. This is not true. Many people who drive expensive cars and wear expensive suits with all the bling have almost no money in their bank accounts. This happens because it is far too easy to spend money.

Many people are making good money. They are rich for a short time until they spend all that they have. Earning it is easier than saving it and multiplying it.

Have you ever seen one rich person who was dumb? No. Students always think they understand more than their professors. A sergeant considers himself smarter than the major. Sometimes it's easier to find a common language with the general than with the sergeant who stands on the street. It almost always happens this way. Why? Because small people always require confirmation of their importance.

Therefore, you need to create a goose that will lay the golden eggs. Try to calculate how much money you need per month so that you can live well, but do not show off. This amount should stay the same, even if your income increases several times.

At one of my training classes, one of the attendees was a modest woman. She came to all of my training and studied well and with great passion. When I asked her how much she earned per month, she calmly replied, "Ten thousand tenge," which is about $31. I was shocked! Then I asked where she got the money for my seminars. She explained that she understood, even at the first stage, that something must be done to improve her life. She had taken a loan to buy a washing machine but instead used the money to invest in her studies. She invested in herself.

You cannot compare that with anything, including that of contributing to your children's education. Think about it . . . why are some people so disappointed in their kids? They scrimped and saved to put the money toward their child's education. The child grows up and says, "What did you do that was so special?! It seems to me that is the exact same thing the other parents did for their kids." The kids did not appreciate the dedication and sacrifices that their parents made to educate them. They thought it was owed to them and that was the way it was supposed to be. That's why the best investment is an investment in yourself.

Hearing this, some parents are disappointed. There is no comparison in the world like an investment in yourself. In the real world, there are two main things that you will never regret —prayer and self-respect. No one can steal those things from you, and they will always stay with you. I know that there are people who live on $200 a month. Try to determine the amount on which you can live for a month. Then try to create your financial plan (the goose that lays the golden eggs). All your previous plans were focused on what to spend. Now you will know the difference between a real financial plan and a spending plan.

FINANCIAL PROTECTION

Take, for example, the figure of $1,000, which an average family can live on for a month (you can use another amount, too). Take the amount, multiply by six, and you get $6,000. This is the figure for six months. So $6,000 is the amount needed to maintain the family for the next six months.

What does this all mean? This means that you will be confident in yourself if you have that amount saved. That confidence means you will not have to worry. You know that no matter what happens—a layoff from work or problems with your health—your family will be able to live for six months just as they do now. You will feel that your family is financially protected during this period.

Some people already had this amount saved a long time ago. But what if you don't have it? Forgo luxuries like cafes, restaurants, alcohol, or cigarettes. Forget about taking the taxi, and cancel your vacation until you save that amount. There is no entertainment and no expensive cosmetics, only food costs and basic necessities. You do not have the right to have fun or relax until you have saved that amount.

Now, multiply $1,000 by twelve months, and it will be $12,000 to cover an entire year. If anyone has that kind of money saved, that's good. For the rest of you, the same rules and restrictions apply, because covering expenses for six months is still not enough. It is better to be safe and save up enough to cover an entire year. During this period, it is possible to regroup . . . to pull yourself together and get another job if you have been laid off. Again, this is financial protection.

A good example is having car or property insurance. Statistics show that those with insured vehicles usually have nothing happen. Ninety percent of all accidents occur with uninsured vehicles. Do you know why? Because when you insure your car or other property, in exchange you get confidence and inner peace. When you insure your material well-being, you will not succumb to the fear of an unstable future.

For example, one woman heard that inflation was coming soon. The inflation would cause prices to increase on everything. She took all her money and bought all sorts of things that could be useful to her in the future. She took them home and hid them. When she returned home from work, she found that the house was completely empty. Burglars had stolen everything. She was in shock! Why did this happen to her? Because in her mind she had a fear of disasters. She was afraid and thus created the unwanted event.

In contrast, insured persons won't have to be stressed out and worried. Their minds are free from doubts and negative feelings. They are relaxed and collected.

When you have accumulated the required amount, place it in a separate bank account without adding more money. Then you will know the exact amount. You may even need to accept the necessity of saving your planned amount and cut your expenses. This is necessary to ensure the financial protection of your family. If your business suddenly starts experiencing difficulties, and, consequently, your revenue falls, you will still be confident. Because should this happen, you can always withdraw money from the account. You will be able to provide your family with everything they need.

Remember that this money has nothing to do with your business and that it is a part of the family budget. The money must be in cash. Do not touch this amount or use it for other frivolous purposes. Make sure that does not happen. If you need to withdraw money from the account, then replace it as quickly as possible.

Money has one property. Let us remember what the Lord wrote in the Bible (Luke 19:26): "Everyone who has will be given more, but from the one who does not have, even what he has will be taken away."

This law works here. When you will accumulate a substantial sum, you will be amazed at how quickly your income will increase. Then you will start to receive new proposals that open up new opportunities. Revenues will grow. Because, after all, it is the law of life.

FINANCIAL SECURITY

Now, take $1,000 (the estimated amount needed to live for a month) and multiply it by 150. You get $150,000.

Remember the mathematical formula, the Pythagorean theorem? This formula is constant and never changes. Likewise, Bodo Schafer set forth a rule for calculating the fixed amount required for financial security. This means that in order to become financially free and provide financial security, you need to gradually accumulate $150,000. This amount will ensure your family's financial security.

If you put this amount in any bank at 8 percent per annum, you will receive $12,000 per year. Divide this interest amount by twelve months, and you get a $1,000 monthly payment. This means that if you accumulate $150,000, you are one of the people who have achieved financial security. Even if you do not work for the rest of your life, you can take the interest accrued and live a normal life! Why is this important?

First, you become financially protected because you saved $12,000.

After that, you start to accumulate the next $150,000. With

this amount of money in your account, you have become financially secure. You may now live without working and receive $1,000 each month from the bank.

Now try to answer this question: "If you knew these rules five years ago, would you have taken advantage of them, and could you have become financially secure?"

Yes or no?

Many people cannot even mentally allow themselves to become rich. They cannot think like rich people. Therefore, I am telling you how to "manage money," not how to "earn it." Because preparation comes first. You need to prepare the soil in order to sow the seeds. If you throw the seeds directly on the pavement, they never grow.

When I first heard about these rules, I thought that maybe in about twenty years, if I set money aside and saved, I would accumulate the $150,000 that I needed to be secure. I really thought that it would take that long to collect and save that much. However, I worked hard, with a goal in mind, and after one and a half months, I became financially protected.

I was amazed.

Over the next eight months, I became financially secure. I myself could not understand how this happened. I could not imagine that everything would happen so quickly. That's when I came to understand the words "start doing and the whole universe will help you."

Believe me, it really does.

God loves creative, self-motivated, successful people. For them, he works wonders. He does not like the sluggish, passive, insecure whiners. A strong wind easily breaks the weak plants and tender shoots. Everything that stops, stops growing, stops moving, and stops living. Herbs, flowers, animals. Even the creek without movement turns into a swamp.

Likewise, the Lord begins to help you when you start to do something. If your activity brings at least one person success and improves his or her quality of life, then destiny starts to help you.

Ask rich people how they became so rich. Many of them will say, "I'll be honest; I cannot explain it. It was simple. I started working, and everything worked out."

In the 1970s, a new company was created by five students. They gathered together and agreed to found the company, but they initially did not know where to start. It took two years to develop ideas.

One of them came up with T-shirts with the logo, and everyone in the company started to wear them. For many years, people all over the world were wearing shirts with the inscription "Just Do It."

You all know this company. It is the manufacturer of sportswear, NIKE. In five to seven years, this manufacturer overtook many well-known companies. Its secret to success was simple: think and do it. The result was one of the largest and most successful companies in the world. So drop the doubts and start acting, and success will be with you. Do not say that you are too old. Do not say that there is no start-up capital, that the legislation is unfavorable for businesses, or that your family circumstances prevent it. Do not look for excuses for inaction.

You can always find excuses; however, your life will not change from all the reasons why you believe you didn't succeed. Isn't it better to make the decision and start moving towards your dream? Try to convince yourself of this. Then begin to act.

I have many examples of people who, after participating in my seminars, implemented all the principles and rules they learned. They have increased their income by 20 to 50 percent over a two-month period. Therefore, do not take everything described in the book as just information. Take it as a life experience. It is like a map helping you to find a direct path to your goals and keeping you off the trails that lead nowhere.

If you achieve financial security, you will be able to live on the passive income of your investment. This does not mean that you no longer need to work. There is yet another step ahead of you.

FINANCIAL FREEDOM

What do you think? How much money do you need to live well? To buy what you want to buy (within reason), to go to cafes and restaurants, or perhaps to take a vacation to the Caribbean? Suppose $10,000 per month. Is this a large amount in your eyes? You should feel as if you already have this amount. You must be convinced that you are worthy of such a life. You do not have to doubt your abilities.

You might think, *Why would I behave this way? I will not become richer.*

I say that you will become richer if you simply believe in yourself!

Now, let's multiply the $10,000 by 150. We get 1.5 million dollars. This amount is not as big as it seems, believe me. If you have a nice house or you have inherited a large house, you are already wealthy.

Life has become better; there are more opportunities to earn decent money. The ability to become rich is now available to virtually everyone. So do not complain about the difficult circumstances. Do not use unfavorable market conditions, high taxes, and the global crisis as an excuse. Remember, it all depends on you.

When you accumulate the amounts of money we discussed, you will have gained financial freedom. This means that by putting money in the bank at 8 percent, you will have an income of $120,000 a year. Divide that up for twelve months and you get a $10,000 per month net income; that will allow you to approach the future with confidence, not fear.

The money will work for you rather than you working for the money. A lot of people do it that way. Why don't you join the community of the wealthy and successful? You will succeed, and you will become a different person. You will feel rich and say, "Yes, I am rich. I am free and relaxed. Now, I do not think about the money. I am now at ease."

You can achieve prosperity in five to seven years. It will be a reality. However, it will only be a reality if your heart and your mind move in the same direction. If you are ready, fight for yourself and for your family who loves you. When this happens, you will feel confident and emotionally satisfied.

Consider this anecdote.

A taxi driver drove a wealthy passenger to his home. When they arrived, he asked the taxi driver how much the fare was. The driver replied, "One hundred dollars."

The passenger was surprised at the amount. "Why is it so expensive?"

The taxi driver replied, "Yesterday, I picked up your son, and he paid me two hundred dollars."

Upon hearing this, the passenger said, "Yes, I understand, but his father is a millionaire, and I'm an orphan."

The point is, the rich understand about money, how they made it, and how they should spend it.

Scientists conducted a study in which they took four monkeys, put them in a cage, and hung bananas from the top. When the monkeys wanted a banana, they started jumping to get to the bananas, and the scientists squirted them with cold water. After a while, the monkeys decided to try again. Once again, they started jumping, and once again the scientists squirted the monkeys with cold water.

Not surprisingly, the time soon came when the monkeys simply looked at the bananas—they were afraid to jump. The scientists placed a new monkey in the cage who did not know anything about the water. She tried to get a banana; however, the other monkeys stopped her and even beat her. After a period of time, another monkey was added to the cage. She also desired a banana. She was stopped and beaten. This happened to each new monkey the scientists placed in the cage. This happened until there were twelve monkeys in the cage.

The researchers removed the first four monkeys from the cage, those who knew from personal experience about the water. Then the next four, who were beaten by the first four, were removed from the cage. This left the last four monkeys placed in the cage.

Afterward, the scientists began to add new monkeys to the cage in the hope they would behave differently. But the scenario was repeated time after time. The newbie monkeys were beaten again, preventing them from jumping to get the bananas. Now, however, the monkeys educating the others did not know about being squirted with cold water. They formed a firm understanding that bananas cannot be touched. Even without knowing the reasons for the ban, they still interfered with other monkeys who wanted to jump for the bananas.

Similar patterns exist in our human world. If you want to achieve something, someone will interfere, because that is what is accepted. The reason for this can be negative information that people around you have heard somewhere. Or it could be from someone's negative experience. People will say a lot of unpleasant things to dissuade you and explain that whatever you are trying to accomplish is not possible.

The takeaway? Brace yourself, believe in yourself, and do not give in to persuasion.

INVESTMENT RULES

Now let's talk about how best to invest.

We are victims of external information. Some of it is true, some is not. For example, how do you know that the Earth is round? You have not seen it yourself; it is what someone else told you. Everyone knows that smoking is harmful. This information affects the decision about whether or not to smoke. Information is the basis for decision making.

When you sit on a chair, it is very stable because it has four legs. A house rests on four load-bearing walls. This is the optimal number of control points. If you remove one leg from the chair, it is possible that it will remain upright, but it will not be stable. Therefore, your money should be invested in four directions.

If you have ever been in the mountains, have you seen how the river collects water from all the small streams adjacent to it? It is through these little streams that it is transformed from a small creek into a turbulent, irrepressible mountain river.

The same principle applies to the financial sector. Having only one source of income, you will never become rich. Therefore, do not work only for one salary. Create cash streams which stack into one cash flow, and they will make you wealthy and successful. Even a college degree won't guarantee that you can become rich. One salaried job is not going to make you rich.

In the past, everyone lived on a salary. It was enough to live on, and possibly a little could be set aside and placed in the bank. Nobody thought about wealth at that time. In today's market-driven economy, it is necessary to move to a new level of understanding of wealth and prosperity.

To protect yourself from downturns and the risks of default, it is necessary to create a cash flow consisting of a variety of different sources of income. A river is a perfect example. It shows how small financial streams can combine to turn into a large river of prosperity. To accomplish this, you must learn to manage money wisely.

Water is a very instructive example. Water has properties that are unique. It has no color, no continuous form, can change states (solid, liquid, or gas), easily takes the shape of any vessel, and can dissolve many substances. Water exhibits softness, but it can also destroy dams, bridges, houses, and can even sharpen stones; therefore, it has great strength. The river gives life to plants and animals living on its banks.

Wealth should be like a river. It absorbs from various sources, and it gives to all the ability to thrive and prosper.

M. S. Norbekov says, "Do not squeeze your fingers into a fist. Keep your hand open and your fingers apart. What fits in the palm of your hand will be yours. With your fingers apart, part of what you receive will fall through them. This will be for others. Your parents, your loved ones and those in need. What is left in your hand, you need to shake and blow on it. Now, the remainder is yours. It will make you rich because the river gives life to all living creatures in its path."

Money will return to the hands of those who know what to do with it. Always consider the interests of your investors and your partners. By knowing their interests, you will be able to formulate a proposal that interests them.

First of all, always learn the plans, intentions, and challenges of your investors. Let your suggestions be the solutions to their problems; then they will agree and say yes.

FOUR STREAMS OF INCOME

For stability, it is necessary to invest in the following four areas, each of which has its own goals and abilities.

1. Cash.

2. Stocks/Bonds.

3. Real Estate.

4. Business.

STREAMS OF INCOME

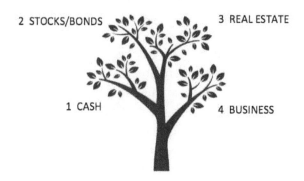

The first investment tool is the cash that you have saved in the bank. It cannot be touched and cannot be removed from the account for any reason, because it provides you with financial protection. The amount will constantly grow thanks to accruing interest.

The second investment strategy involves stocks and bonds. It is not difficult to do. At first glance, it all seems very complicated and confusing. Simply learn and try to understand all you can. Buy shares on the stock exchange. It is better if you start doing this in small amounts. If the price of the shares should fall suddenly, nothing terrible will happen, but you will gain experience.

Over time, you will learn how to assess the situation: buying and selling at the right time, investing in safe stocks, and making money on the price jumps. For those who know how to assess the situation, there is an interesting rule—they buy stocks when everyone else is afraid to do so, and they sell when everyone else wants to buy.

The third investment opportunity is real estate. Real property always has value, is easy to sell, and can generate a steady cash flow. Real estate has long been considered a profitable investment. If you decide to buy a house or an apartment, buy it from successful people. Even if you buy clothes, watches, shoes, etc., buy them in reputable stores, not where they are cheapest. People usually say, "At the market (flea market or bazaar), I can buy something a lot cheaper."

But you need to pay for everything. Buying is more expensive in the salon; however, you are just paying the money. Even if you're able to buy something cheaper at the market, you will spend your time looking for what you need. The money can be returned, earning you more money. However, your time is gone forever.

The essence of our principles is to become successful without increasing the number of hours spent at work, without increasing your working day. Therefore, all of our training is aimed at saving time . . . the ability to manage time and use it wisely. I repeat: it is better to work hard for three to five years to be able to enjoy the rest of your life. Then you can work at your pleasure and live a normal life.

When you buy a property, try to buy it from successful people. "Why?" you ask. Even the walls of the apartment literally absorb all the negative energy of the owners, quarrels, nervous breakdowns, bad moods, and negative emotions.

It is better to overpay a little bit to buy a home from affluent people than to save money trying to be stingy. Your family's happiness, your children's health, and harmony in the family mean more than money. Money can always be returned. A wall, and even other things around it, tends to accumulate the negative energy of its owners, including their problems and failures. Therefore, be careful not to quarrel at home.

When you save money and buy something cheaper, it can have negative implications on other aspects of your life. Even if you are buying property for resale, a "cheap buy" cannot bring the desired profit. If it does, the money will drain like water through your fingers.

Generally, it is best to buy a new apartment or build your

own home from scratch, because then you put in your positive emotions. Your hopes and dreams are in the house. You're imagining how you will live in it—how you will divide the rooms, arrange the furniture, and decorate the walls of your home with a positive energy. Therefore, it is better to build or buy new homes or apartments.

The fourth investment goal is to become part of a company—to acquire a patent, copyright, license, or insurance policy, or to make direct investments in promising companies. You can do this by investing some of your money into company projects. Or you can buy several insurance policies. It is desirable to have them long term since they gain value. They will give you confidence and ensure your future.

You cannot simply invest in one of the four investment strategies because there is always a certain risk. Only contributions to all four areas guarantee you financial independence and security.

LIFE GOALS

Have a goal for your whole life, a goal for one section of your life, a goal for a shorter period and a goal for the year; a goal for every month, a goal for every week, a goal for every day, a goal for every hour and for every minute, and sacrifice the lesser goal to the greater.

~ LEO TOLSTOY

Many people live to be up to eighty or ninety years old, but they still do not have a clue about their goals in life. Life is given to us only once. We should make life more intense, beautiful, and rich, both spiritually and materially. Every morning we need to think about our goals.

My mentor asked a soldier, who had been discharged from the military, where he had served. He replied that he was lucky. He was attached to the soldier's kitchen where he worked. People standing nearby heard his answer, too. They roared with approval, believing that he really was lucky.

At that moment, I thought the same thing; however, my mentor said, "Remember, life is too short to spend two years peeling potatoes. In the army, you can learn a lot. You can acquire useful skills, get rid of some weaknesses, grow and mature. Spending that much time in the kitchen is too wasteful." It is clear that people are looking for the easier path, but that is only an excuse for their weaknesses.

Never waste your time on unnecessary things. Otherwise, in the most important moment, you may not have enough time, a few hours or even minutes, to realize your dream.

Narrow down your goals. They should be written down clearly and concisely; however, you need to list realistic goals. Do not list all your goals, because it will overwhelm you. If you look at your dreams from the position of what you earn, listing all your goals can seem impossible, and you will give up. You will lose your confidence and simply set aside taking action until better times. It is better to divide the big goals into small ones. Then it will be easier for you to achieve them. You can go from one small goal to another, gradually approaching the most important thing. In the beginning, it will be easier, knowing that the first goal is attainable. That will give you the confidence to achieve the entire chain, leading to your big dream.

Why do so many people fail to achieve their goals? They focus on their big goals and get overwhelmed. Yes, your big goals are worthy of being the main focus. But you can see them and think that they are not realistic. Don't say you have four big goals. Your mind does not distinguish between large and small targets; it responds to the volume. Think about money: if you didn't see the numbers on the bills, your consciousness wouldn't comprehend a single bill for one million dollars since it is only one bill. But if you see two hundred one hundred-dollar bills, that will excite the consciousness, because it responds to the volume.

For example, a child cannot understand when we say, "This is an expensive toy." The child perceives the amount or volume, a lot of toys or only one. They do not understand adult explanations that the toy is expensive or cheap. The same principle applies to your consciousness . . . visual perception is important; it reacts when it sees a lot of money.

Suppose you want to open a large manufacturing plant. Yes, this is a global goal. You don't know what to do to open a factory. You do not know where to start. If you write a business plan, it will then be easy to see all your steps. You must make the financial model, calculate all the expenses, and figure out the return on your investment.

Remember: if you approach investors and tell them about your idea, they will look at you and smile. Then they will ask for a concrete business plan and plan of action. If you go to the bank with your idea and ask for a loan, they will require a business plan. Nobody wants to invest in a vague idea. Therefore, first you must learn how to make a detailed business plan.

Large companies have managers and directors that take care of the daily tasks. Directors place their signatures on documents that have been prepared for them even though they may not be competent in the intricacies of management. On the other hand, managers clearly understand the big picture—industry pros and cons, current issues facing the company, and the staff's strengths and weaknesses. If directors are fired, they run the risk of remaining unemployed. When managers are fired, they understand that their skillset is valuable and they will be able to get another job. After all, the world needs talented and competent people. If you are a professional and enjoy your work, any director will take you into his or her company as a trusted hire.

A good example of this is Lee Iacocca. Iacocca had a long run at Ford, one of the largest automobile corporations in the world. Then he was fired. After his dismissal at Ford, he was hired by Chrysler, another American auto giant. There Iacocca demonstrated his extraordinary management skills. He was able to raise Chrysler to a new level. When Ford fired Iacocca, they lost a talented manager.

Good managers are demanding. They are also fair. They oversee the discipline and implementation of planned tasks, create optimal conditions for each employee, and coordinate the work of all the structures. They are able to get along with people and clearly delineate the work of the entire enterprise.

If you are a good dad, your son will follow your example. If you are a manager, but are not able to manage even yourself, no one will trust you.

Managers always start with themselves. If you tell your son that you are a good dad, he may smile because he knows your weaknesses. Children tend to mimic their parents, including copying their flaws.

If you look at a river from the ground, it may seem that it flows straight without twists and turns. If you look at it from an airplane, you can see that the river flows and meanders. This is because it bypasses the obstacles in its path.

People can likewise overcome or bypass the obstacles to their goals. You can specifically avoid obstacles in your way to keep moving in the right direction. This is what managers can do to help you reach a goal. They direct the "flow" in the right path. In the same way that we treat ourselves, we manage our thoughts, emotions, motives, and actions to realize our dreams. The way we do it, how we relate to our goals, and the result all depend on what we do.

Our ability to govern ourselves, to think, to notice, to force ourselves to carry out our plan, and to refrain from negative feelings determines the degree of the reality of our plans. Socrates said, "Lazy is not only the person who does nothing, but also the person who can do better, but doesn't."

Who do you think is the best lawyer? The one who knows a lot about the law or the one who may find a good argument and evidence when it is needed? Is the wisest person someone who knows a lot or someone who uses his or her knowledge at the right time? There is a difference.

Therefore, always try to be the manager. When you do something for yourself or work on yourself, do it with love, with respect for yourself—not because life requires, or even forces, you to do something.

If something in your life is not working, unless you have enough perseverance, attentiveness, willpower, and patience, do not rush to blame yourself. On the basis of psychogenetics I can say perhaps that the possible reason why your life is not working is hidden in your genes. Do not worry, though, since the reason is open to correction. The main thing is that you need to work on yourself. You need to correct your shortcomings. For this to happen, it is necessary to realize that you can change yourself for the better. Then begin to work on yourself.

Desire creates thoughts, and thoughts generate action. Sometimes people say, "I really wanted to, but I couldn't." It is not true. If you want it, if it is something that you passionately wish, then you will achieve it.

DOUBTS

One of the worst traits in a person is constant doubt. When you buy something, you are in doubt. What if the salesperson is lying and trying to rip you off? Remember: by worrying about this scenario, it often turns out that way. Because of that salesperson's dishonesty, we shape the future. Maybe with another customer, that salesperson would have acted honestly. But he or she will trick you because of your constant doubt and uncertainty. Your doubts led that salesperson to cheat you. So never hesitate to trust the people around you; trust them to do the right thing.

When I opened my own company, I placed an ad: "I will hire the best." They gathered, those people who were the best. Plan to select only the best people and work with the best experts in their fields.

Many people are skeptical when they hear about the best deals. They fear that the money will not come back. Wealth is not something that you have at the moment; wealth must constantly work for you and multiply. Otherwise you run the risk of losing it forever.

PARABLE OF "DOUBT"

One poor man lived by begging, knocking on the doors of the city's residents. Once he saw a golden carriage starting to enter the city. In the carriage sat a majestic king, beaming with a radiant smile.

The beggar said to himself, "My struggles and my poor life are over! This king with a beaming face came to the city because of me. I know that he will give me his riches, and I will live in peace."

As if to confirm his thoughts, by order of the king, the carriage stopped. The beggar watched, ran down, climbed up, and looked at the king, convinced that this was his lucky break.

Then the king held out his hand to the beggar and said, "What do you have to give me?"

Surprised and taken aback, the beggar did not know what to say. He thought, *What is this, some kind of a game that the king is offering to play? Is he kidding me?*

Not understanding the king's true motives, the beggar

doubted the sincerity of the king and was confused. But seeing that the king, still smiling, did not lower his outstretched hand, the beggar reached into his knapsack, which contained a few pinches of rice. He took one grain of rice and placed it on the palm of the king's hand. The king thanked him and ordered the driver to continue his journey. The horses carried the gold carriage away.

At the end of the day, the beggar pulled the remains of the rice from his knapsack. He found one golden grain among all the grains of rice. Then he started crying, wailing, "Why did I not give all my rice?"

Notes

CHAPTER 7

HOW TO ENJOY MONEY

Pleasure is the happiness of fools,
happiness is the pleasure of wise.
~ Jules Barbey d'Aurevilly

We often spend money on things that are not absolutely
necessary. When making an investment, we rationalize our
fears, arguing to ourselves that even though the investment
only pays a small percentage, our money is safe. It is clear that
when persons invest, they may lose their money. It is better to
strive for freedom, not just for safety, if you want to become
financially free. Play the money game not to lose, but rather
to win. Set aside what you can and invest in your future. Do
not say, "I am already fifty or sixty years old, and I don't need
money." Do not count the years, but rather the moments that
make you happy. Invest in your future.

Where should you invest? What things are really important?

1. Charity.

2. What did you do with your chance in life?

3. Skills and abilities.

4. Hobbies and fun.

Life is not counted by years, but rather is counted by minutes of real joy from the results of your own work. Many of us live better than our neighbors and relatives. And, of course, better than our ancestors. Now we have a better chance of success. That money determines which level you have achieved. For some people, it is very low.

Try to determine your level for yourself. The world has changed in the last twenty years, and new opportunities have appeared. But some people continue to live in the past. How can you reach a point where you can enjoy the money? I will teach you so that you become happy, successful, and rich instead of just having money but not enjoying life. I have seen poor people who were happy and rich people who were unhappy.

CHARITY

There are many people in the world who are needy. The best feature of the rich is the desire to help others. Persons who think that they will manage without ever receiving help from others are very mistaken. However, those who think that others will manage without their help are mistaken twice.

To enjoy your money, you need to give something to the world, to people in need. Traditionally, Muslims should give 2.5 percent of their income to charity. Christians tithe up to 10 percent or more. Some people say, "I don't have enough money for myself now; however, when I'm rich, I will give for sure." This is self-deception. If you currently cannot pay 2.5 percent or 10 percent of $100, then when you have $1 million, you are more unlikely to give, because it will be a much larger amount.

Therefore, give this percentage, no matter how much you have now. It does not matter if it is $10 or $1; give 25 cents even. From now on, this needs to be the rule.

At the same time, remember that if you are greedy and do not give, life will take your money several times more. It will do this through inflation, sickness, and through your own confusion, but it will still take it. When you do not give, you also do not receive.

In 2 Corinthians 9:7, the Bible says, "Each of you should give what you have decided in your heart to give, not reluctantly or under compulsion, for God loves a cheerful giver." It is also written in the Bible that "A generous person will prosper." And it is so.

WHAT DO YOU DO WITH YOUR CHANCE IN LIFE?

Someone once said that poverty is a luxury. What type of nervous system do you need to have to endure hardship, what willpower do you need to justify your unenviable condition, when you see successful and wealthy people around you?!

Poverty is a legacy.

If children live in poverty, they see poverty as a normal, acceptable position in life. They do not have a good example to follow. Our children are not guilty if the way we live today is not the way we wanted to live. We need to give them a better life. It is always easier to find an excuse for your position than to try to change something.

When I left my village, my mother asked me where I was going. I said I did not want to spend my whole life there in the village, that I considered myself worthy of seeing the whole world. To which she replied, "Stay, and all the property which

SAID DAVLATOV

I gained in my life will be yours." I looked around and saw a little house, 500 square meters of land (0.12 of an acre), livestock, and every little thing she was generously offering me.

It wasn't what I was looking for.

Life in the village was monotonous. In the summer, I mowed and dried grass, and during the winter I fed it to my mother's livestock. In the fall, I sold excess livestock and bought necessary things. It was not the worst way of life. After all, many people who live in the city are bound by routine, too, just in a different way: they go to work every day, sit at a desk all day, and in the evening come home to the TV. It turns out the same, with minor differences for the urban lifestyle.

When I left my native village, my mother was crying, not wanting to let me go. I firmly said that I wanted to change something in my life: I wanted to see the world. I wanted to seize the opportunity given to me by the universe.

My mentor told me that the whole world was created for me, and that I had to prepare myself to be ready to take what I wanted. However, at the same time, we have to remember that nothing belongs to us, not even our bodies, because we cannot take it with us when we pass away. This understanding will help you not to be selfish.

A wise man once said to his children, "Honor, respect, and courage make you a king, wherever you may be, but not all kings have these qualities." Whoever you are, wherever you are, whatever you do, always remember the rule: believe in God and be honest with yourself.

Consider the parable of chance.

A man woke up one night and saw an angel. The angel told the man that he could expect a bright future: he would have the opportunity to become rich, to achieve respect in society, and to marry a beautiful woman. The man lived his life waiting for the promised blessings, but nothing good ever happened. He died poor and alone.

When he went up to the gates of heaven, he saw that same angel, the one who had promised him wealth during his lifetime. The man became angry.

"Angel, you promised me wealth, universal respect, and a beautiful wife. I have spent a lifetime waiting for all this, but none of it has come true!"

"I did not give you such a promise," the angel said. "I promised that you would have the *opportunity* to become rich, respected, and loved."

The man was surprised. "I do not understand what you mean by that."

"Do you remember how once you had the idea of creating your own business, but because of fear of defeat you refused, and never tried to implement it?"

The man nodded.

"A few years later," the angel continued, "the same idea occurred to another person, and he was not afraid of failure. Remember, he became one of the richest people in the country!

"You must also remember a terrible earthquake that destroyed the city to the ground. Thousands of people remained under the rubble of houses. At that time, you had the chance to participate in the search for the missing and rescue survivors from the rubble. You did not want to leave your house for fear that looters would ransack it. So you ignored calls for help and stayed at home."

The man felt a burning shame, then nodded.

"This was your chance," the angel said, "to save the lives of hundreds of people and gain their respect.

"Finally, do you remember a beautiful woman with red hair that you liked so much? You found her incomparable, but you thought that this woman would not marry you. In order to avoid rejection, you did not offer anything."

The man nodded again, but now the tears were rolling

down his cheeks.

The angel looked at the man and said, "Yes, my friend, she could have been your wife. She would have been happy with you, and you would have had beautiful, healthy children, and your name would have flourished."

All of us are given opportunities on a daily basis; however, because of our fears and our indecision, we often do not take advantage of those chances.

SKILLS AND ABILITIES

Then there's this story.

There was a young man who had a good voice. The young man loved to sing. He enjoyed speaking in front of audiences. He dreamed that someday he would be singing at the famous opera house La Scala in Milan, where celebrities perform. After the young singer received his musical education, he had to travel around the country giving performances to earn a living.

In one city the young man was in between performances when he was approached by an old friend, who had not seen the singer for a long time. The friend asked, "What are you doing here?" The young man replied that he sang to provide for his family. The friend said, "I'm not talking about that; what are you *doing* here?"

"I'm telling you that I work to provide for my family!" the singer exclaimed in surprise.

The friend said, "No, I'm not talking about that. What did you do with the chance that life gave you to realize your dreams?"

Every person has some kind of talent. This talent is given to you so that you can bring people joy. By realizing this talent, you achieve success, recognition, and, of course, well-being. The singer, after the conversation with his longtime friend, could not find a place for himself. He was bitter, and he drank. The next time he went on stage, he began to sing, forgetting everything in the world. He sang with all the passion of which only he was capable. When he finished, the audience gave him a standing ovation. The theater director appreciated the magnificent singing and immediately offered the talented young man a permanent job. But he refused, saying that he would go for his dream.

It was Enrico Caruso, the famous opera singer.

Do not waste your chance, the chance which is given to each person. Try to remember that money comes to the one who realizes his talents. Do not squander your ability to earn a living. Realizing your talent, you embody your dreams and become financially independent. Use the slightest chance which provides you your destiny. Only then will you be happy.

Scientists once conducted a study on the topic "What is happiness?" They came to the conclusion that happiness is something that does not belong only to you. You are happy when you give joy, inspiration, hope, and kindness to others. From this giving, happiness is not reduced; it is multiplied.

HOBBIES AND FUN

As you go through life and travel on your journey to earn and save, don't forget to have fun in the process.

Always leave time for relaxation and activities that bring pleasure. The best advice that I was given by a mentor was if within three years, your work has not given you the way of life which you dreamed of, then you should quit the job. If it did not raise you to a new level, either spiritually or materially, or if you have not achieved any tangible results to be proud of, leave that job.

As Avicenna said, "You are not a tree that you will stay in the same spot." Also, in the words of Jim Rohn, "If you don't like how things are, change it! You're not a tree."

If nobody can understand you in your current situation, why waste your life trying to prove to someone that your opinions and beliefs are correct? It is better to just leave. There is no need to stay where you do not want to be. Maybe another door is open to you somewhere else.

Sure, you can stay where you are and wait. However, when you finally decide to change your life—or life forces you to make a drastic change—you may find that the other door is now closed. Someone else took advantage of that opportunity, and it is now lost to you.

Of course, you can make the excuse, "I knew that it would be this way. I left that job for nothing. I was already adjusted to it and had a paycheck. Even though the pay was small, I had money. And there was no guarantee that the new job would have been better."

So say people who want to be in the process. The result is not important to them.

Do you understand now how to enjoy money? I hope you do. Money only brings you happiness and success when it fulfills all the dimensions of your character. Money is a catalyst for happiness and cannot be the goal. It should bring joy, confidence, and a desire to help others. It should create conditions for the realization of your abilities and the talents of your children. You have to live a life rich with positive emotions. That is the main thing.

NOTES

CHAPTER 8

OBSTACLES

It is not in the still calm of life, or the repose of a pacific station, that great characters are formed. The habits of a vigorous mind are formed in contending with difficulties.
~ABIGAIL ADAMS

Everyone thinks that the key to success is to make more money. There is a system required in order to be successful. Whether you fail or succeed, you can still learn and you can still become successful and wealthy. How?

1. Repetition.

2. Philosophy of the ant.

3. How to handle rejection.

4. Problems.

5. Accidents and Disasters.

6. Sickness and Disease.

7. Pity.

8. Disappointment.

A gardener caring for trees does not carry water to water the garden. Instead, he clears a ditch, removing the obstacles in the way of the flowing water. The garden begins to bloom and bear fruit. However, there are other obstacles—weeds, insects, or other pests, for example—that can impede the garden's vitality. What obstacles do you face?

Suppose that you offer some sort of item or product. At one point, you are refused. Then you are refused a second and a third time. Gradually you lose confidence in yourself, and you start to doubt the efficiency and quality of your own products.

Maybe you have an idea and you want to implement it. You talk about it to your friend, and the friend says, "Do you consider yourself smarter than others? If this idea had any merit, others would have done it long ago."

You talk about your idea to a second person, such as a close relative. The relative is not too encouraging and points out everything wrong with your idea. Then you talk to a third person. That person only further discourages you, finding your idea unrealistic. Gradually, you lose heart. But your friends and family have never been rich. They are judging from their own experience and therefore give such advice through their own experiential lens. They think that they are protecting you from yourself, showing concern for you and your money.

From all this advice, you gradually lose the desire to realize your idea. You lose confidence in yourself, and you start to doubt and give up your plans. Time passes, and then you suddenly find out that someone succeeded on the idea you gave up on. Your idea came to fruition, but for someone else!

STORY OF PERSEVERANCE

One man was plagued with business failures and went bankrupt in 1831. He failed as a candidate for elections in 1835. His fiancée died in 1835. In 1836, he suffered a nervous breakdown. He lost elections to the US Congress in 1843, 1846, 1848, and 1855. His hopes of becoming the vice president failed to materialize in 1856, and in 1858 he lost an election to the Senate. This man was Abraham Lincoln, and in 1860 he was elected president of the United States of America.

The only person who loses is the one who stops fighting. For the loser, life becomes a graveyard of unused opportunities. Strong persons use all their given opportunities and even create new ones.

REPETITION

I read about an insurance agent who seemingly did the impossible. By nature, he was very indecisive and insecure, and people did not want to do business with him. His coworkers, including management, considered him a "weak" insurance agent. He lived in a small village where everyone knew each other.

In the village was a supermarket, whose owner was a rich man, and he did not give in to anyone. Even the most experienced insurance agents were unable to insure his property.

The insurance agent set a goal to sell insurance to the supermarket owner. Nobody believed he would be able to succeed, and they even laughed at him. However, in order to achieve his goal, the agent practiced. Every morning he went to the park, sat on the bench and said, "You will buy a policy from me, you will buy a policy from me." Afterward, he went to see the supermarket owner. Every time, the owner told him no.

One day, the owner of the supermarket was finally tired of

all the agent's visits. He said, "Look, I'm so tired of you! Don't you understand that I don't want to deal with you?"

Not in the least embarrassed, the insurance agent replied, "I persist because I strive for my dreams."

The owner was curious and asked, "You come here every day to listen to my refusal? I do not understand why you keep coming, knowing that my answer will be no. What do your dreams have to do with it?"

"I'm here training myself every day," the agent calmly replied.

"How do you train here?" asked the owner, intrigued.

The agent explained, "When I come to you and get a refusal, I convince myself that my desire to realize my dream remains the same. I do not want to lose faith in myself, and therefore I aspire to get a positive result. When I come to you, my desire to become successful keeps growing. After each meeting with you, I leave . . . and I sell at least one policy. I train my persistence and my ability to persuade. After seeing you, everything turns out fine."

The supermarket owner looked at him in surprise and thought for a few minutes. Then he offered to buy an insurance policy. It was for an amount that he, the agent, and the other agents could only dream of.

How did the agent accomplish the impossible? He did so because of the recurrence rule. Studies have shown that when you are presenting something for the first time, you have a 95 percent guarantee that you will be rejected. The motivation here is simple. You thought over everything very well, weighed your options, and then presented the offer. Your client heard about it for the first time, and that's why it was difficult for him to make a decision.

Remember how your neurons work? A stable relationship between the neurons is produced by repetition. With repetition, the neurons form a set stereotype (pattern) of perception. Therefore, regardless of their desire, over time, your client will think about your offer.

Remember, in the recent past, in the days of the Soviet Union or the revolutionary war, people were ready to give their lives for an idea, for the motherland. Patriotic education formed the real defenders of the motherland. People were ready to sacrifice their lives, imagining at the same time what people would say about them in the future: "They gave their lives for a cause."

We all dreamed at that time of performing a heroic feat. The path of human consciousness formed a steady pattern of thinking. Any repetition was deposited in the human mind.

This rule applies to business as well. As the saying goes: "If a person repeats ten times to someone that the person is a dog, on the eleventh time that person will bark." Therefore, when you first come to someone with a proposal, that person is not ready to perceive your ideas. When you approach that person a second time, you have an 80 percent chance you will be rejected. The third time, this figure (the probability of a negative response) is reduced to 70 percent. It is only on the ninth time that you have a 95 percent guarantee of your success.

Therefore, when you once again get rejected, say to yourself, "How great it is that the probability of failure is further reduced by 10 percent. The next time, the chance of getting a positive response will be greater."

Holding your head high, move on. Always remember that with every rejection you experience, you climb one step closer to victory. In addition, every time this happens, you increase your skill and professionalism.

Persons who do not know these principles will lose confidence with each failure and may give up, abandoning their dreams. Knowledge of these principles will help you achieve good results. The principles form a pattern derived from the experiences of successful people. Your knowledge will definitely lead you to success. Never stop halfway to your goal. Keep trying again and again.

A good example of someone with incredible persistence is Thomas Edison. He was a person who did not lose heart, and even with failure after failure, he achieved impressive results.

Working to develop his next invention, Edison experimented five hundred times, experiencing defeat after defeat. Nobody believed in the success. All his staff had quit, and only one of his students remained.

The student said to Edison, "Master, we've tried to do it five hundred times, but nothing has happened, and all the staff have quit. Yet every day you come with this spirit and enthusiasm, as if everything is going well."

Edison smiled and replied, "But, in fact, things are going well: they're going great."

The student did not understand Edison's optimism and turned to him with another question. "Can you explain to me why you think that things are going well?"

"Think about it," Edison replied. "We have discovered five hundred ways that do not work!"

Optimists always focus on the future, on a positive result, and believe in success. This helps them achieve their goals.

PHILOSOPHY OF THE ANT

Anyone who has tried to stop an ant knows about the ant's dedication and perseverance. No obstacle can stop him. He climbs over and goes around, but he will find a way to go even further. Try to put a brick in his path. When he sees an obstacle, he will immediately start to look for a solution. The ant never accepts defeat and always strives toward his goal.

When an ant finds a small seed or a crumb of bread, he will try to carry the find to the anthill. At the same time, none of the other ants will rush to take his bounty away. In fact, it's quite the contrary—other ants will come to help and work together to deliver the food to the nest.

Ants are the most numerous insects on the ground. There are sixteen million species, and for each person on the planet, there are about twenty billion ants. The ant is very industrious and works from early morning until late evening. When a man comes home from work tired and sits down to rest, the ant is not even thinking about rest. He continues to work. When the man wakes up, no matter how early in the morning, the ant is already working.

Be observant. The best teacher is nature. It gives us a striking example of hard work, harmony, and beauty. If you want a good example of persistence and diligence, take a picture of an ant. Hang pictures of the ant on the wall at home and at work. They will remind you and your staff to always pursue your goals, no matter what the obstacles. And remember, the smart say what they want to do, the wise say what they have done, and the fools will talk about both.

HOW TO HANDLE REJECTION

Upon his departure, Jesus left two rules for his students. Remember these rules and try to be guided by them in your lives.

1. *Always be in pairs, go together, communicate together; the two of you are a lot stronger than one.*

If we have two cables, and each one is capable of handling a load of ten tons, how many tons can they handle together?

Do you think it is twenty tons?

The answer is no. Combined, they can handle a weight of thirty tons. Together, they can withstand more than each alone.

It is the same way in life.

Alexander the Great knew about this. His teacher, Aristotle, said that respect and understanding between two men could solve impossible tasks. Alexander proved it by conquering half the world when he was only twenty-four years old. The combined efforts of two or more people lead to greater results.

Consider a family in which the husband and wife love, respect, and understand each other. They will achieve a lot more together. We all have similar examples when a close family, starting from scratch, gradually achieves financial success and becomes wealthy. This is the most effective force, the force of mutual understanding and respect. Even in those days, when there was no general education, Jesus already knew the truth and tried to bring it to the people.

Together you are stronger—remember this.

2. *The second rule is also very important to understand and accept. Matthew 10:14 says, "And whosoever shall not receive you, nor hear your words, when ye depart out of that house or city, shake off the dust of your feet."*

Therefore, if someone does not want to listen to you, if someone does not accept you in that someone's heart and speaks poorly about you or your affairs, then when you leave his house (or hers), shake off the dust from your feet, continue to do your business, and believe in success.

Sooner or later, some people, even your friends or your family, can hurt you with their comments. They may say that they do not believe in the worthiness of your goals, that your dreams are not possible, or that they doubt your ability to achieve results. Do not take their comments to heart.

Even if your mother said something negative about your wife or if your brother hurt you with his suspicions, simply brushing off your clothes and shoes allows you to remove the negative impact of these words and cleanse your mind of doubt and uncertainty. You leave all the negative words where they were spoken.

You have to believe in your dreams. You must believe in your abilities and move towards your goal. Do not give up on your dreams, even if someone looks at your dreams another way, if your friends or relatives do not support you in your endeavors, or if another person says that your dreams are impossible.

Consider the following parable.

Once upon a time, there lived a sage. He helped people, and they kept coming to him for advice. But there was another wise man who was jealous of his popularity.

One day, the jealous man had an idea for how to humiliate his opponent. He decided that the next day he would bring together all the people on the square. He would ask the sage, so everyone could hear, whether the butterfly in his hand was alive or dead.

He said to himself, "If the sage says that the butterfly is alive, I will crush it, and it will be dead. His answer will be wrong. If the sage says it is dead, then I will open my hand, and the live butterfly will fly away. In either case, his answer will be wrong."

Pleased with his idea, he went to sleep.

The next morning, the jealous man assembled all the people, invited the sage, and asked him, "You know the secrets of life and know all the answers, so answer the easiest one. I have in my hand a butterfly: is it alive or dead?"

Everyone understood the trick and looked at the sage, but he just smiled and replied, "Everything is in your hands. If you grip your fingers, it will die, and if you open your hand, it will fly away."

Just remember, other people's opinions are theirs and theirs alone. Do not allow their attitudes or emotions to change your outlook.

One day, I was approached by a man who asked for help

opening a bakery. It was in Russia. I said to him, "This town is full of bakeries; how are you going to succeed with so many competitors? This is unreal."

He convinced me by replying, "Let there be a hundred bakeries, and mine will be the one hundred and first. All the same, people will come and buy from me. I will succeed, whatever it may cost me."

This is the philosophy of success. Let there be a thousand competitors, but I will still be among the best.

With his confidence and strength of character, I knew he was destined for success. I supported his idea and helped him open the bakery.

The same applies to any of us. If the industry is packed with competitive products, but you are adamant and confident in your abilities, then you will succeed. Willpower and determination help see you through.

PROBLEMS

There is not one person free from problems. Everybody has problems, and there is nowhere to run from them.

Often persons create problems themselves. Then they heroically overcome them. However, if problems are able to stop you, it is better to never even start, because the problems will always be there. Any obstacle can be a reason for you to stop. And that same obstacle can cause you to push forward . . . with an even greater determination!

There are two types of people: The first will stop, failing to overcome even minor obstacles. At heart, these people are always in doubt and nothing can reassure them. Any problem can cause them to reject their dreams. Even bad weather!

The second type of people are quite the opposite. Faced with difficulties, they work with renewed vigor. It is as if the obstacles make them stronger and more determined to succeed.

This is the philosophy of success. Any obstacle can cause your dreams to fail or be a source of even greater desire to achieve your goals. Success depends on you—on your strength of character and your belief in your dreams.

Do not stop when you are faced with problems. Any problem is a test of your strength of character, and what comes easily is cheaply valued. Success is seeking only those who, despite all difficulties, continue towards their goals. You cannot give up your dreams and your goals just because something did not work perfectly the first time. You need to continue until what you desire becomes a reality.

PARABLE OF THE PROBLEM

One Master and one Guardian ran a monastery. They belonged to the Zen sect. The Guardian was very old. Then, one day, he passed away. With his passing, it was necessary to find a successor. The Master called all the students together so that a successor could be chosen from among them.

The Master said, "I will present you with one problem. Whoever solves the problem first will be the new Guardian."

In the center of a bench, the Master placed a beautiful porcelain vase with an exquisite rose in it. He said to the students, "This is the problem."

The students looked upon the vase with awe. They looked at what was before their eyes: the complex and strange drawings on porcelain, the color and shape of the rose petals.

"What does it all mean?" they said to themselves. "What mystery lies behind this? What should I do?"

Everyone was at a loss.

After a few minutes, one student stood up and looked at the Master and the other students. He walked up to the vase, picked it up, raised it above his head and, in front of everyone, smashed it on the floor.

"You will be the new Guardian," the Master said. Then he explained his reasoning to the rest.

"I told you very clearly that this is a problem. No matter how beautiful or tempting it looks, there are problems that exist and need to be solved. They can take the form of a beautiful vase—it can be love, which has already lost its meaning. Or perhaps it's the realization we need to leave, but we don't want to leave, because it gives us convenience and comfort. There is only one way to solve the problem: you have to deal with it face-to-face. In such moments, we cannot afford to show pity or be seduced by attractive parties. They will exist in any conflict."

Problems have one surprising effect which affects the majority of us. We like to have them, to analyze them, to come back to them, and then to talk about them.

Often we compare our problems with the hardships of others, saying that all their problems are nothing compared to ours. Here is our problem and it's really serious. But what is the solution?

ACCIDENTS AND DISASTERS

Thomas Edison, the great inventor, once had his laboratory catch on fire. It was a terrible fire. Everyone ran around in a panic, not knowing what to do, because the laboratory was filled with years of research and experiments. Edison was calm; he even smiled, looking at the fire.

Edison's son was standing next to him. The son thought his father's behavior seemed strange. He could not understand why his father was happy.

When Edison realized his son's reaction, he asked him to call his mother. When she arrived, Edison, who had a very keen sense of humor, asked, "Are you still my wife or not?" His wife answered in the affirmative. Edison said, "Look, darling, what a spectacle. All of our mistakes and errors burned up. Now we can start all over again. "

Wise and powerful people can turn their failures into a source of positive energy. The added difficulties increase their will and determination, and they are motivated to keep going forward.

My advice? Become like them.

SICKNESS AND DISEASE

Do you think that sickness may stop you . . . or not? Do you know when people often get sick? They get sick when there is no interest in life, no inspiration, and no desire to achieve anything. If you have a lot of ideas, you will never get sick, believe me. Money will inspire you so much that you will run after your dreams and not feel your feet.

Remember, the money does not become an end in itself. It becomes a source of financial independence and helps you to realize your talents. If your loved ones get sick, do you stop? When you are sick yourself, that is one thing. When your child is sick, everything is much more complicated. What will happen to your passion and to your dreams?

Be careful never to betray your dreams, no matter what happens, because such betrayal affects your future, your child's future, and the future of all your loved ones. If you stop, there is nothing you can help them with. Your progress determines the well-being of the family.

Arnold Shvets, a successful doctor and friend of mine, said, "No one can stop a person who is able to risk everything to achieve that person's goals." He was forty years old when he dropped everything to go to medical school. He went to America and set up his clinic, which is now known all over the world. He did what he wanted and what he had dreamed about.

PITY

Pity is one of the most difficult obstacles. Do not feel pity for anyone, and this includes *yourself*. Self-pity is a sign of weakness. It will destroy you.

If you see sick persons, do not show that you feel pity towards them, because pity will humiliate them. Which would you rather have? Pity or respect? If it is respect, then go for it: deserve respect.

What would you like? Someone to sympathize with you, or to be loved by someone? If you want to be loved, then you need to love.

Arnold Schwarzenegger said, "Do not feel sorry for yourself if you crave freedom and strive for your dreams."

DISAPPOINTMENT

Try to never be disappointed. If you are unable to avoid disappointment, focus your attention on your dream. This will help you overcome your depressed psychological state and tune in to the positive.

Buddha said, "If you hit a dead end, go back to the beginning of your story."

Sometimes difficulties arise in family relationships. In this case, it is important to find common ground. If your financial situation has crashed and you do not know why, go back to the beginning. If you disappoint someone, or someone has disappointed you, you do not need to assign blame. Go back to the beginning of your relationship and focus on what can be done to rectify the situation.

The greatest disappointment is the betrayal of a very close loved one. That is not easy to overcome. No matter what happens in your life, even if someone closest to you betrays you, do not be discouraged, do not get depressed. Concentrate all your attention on your dream.

If someone lies to you, do not stop. Some people give up their dreams because of someone else's fraud. Then they take out the betrayal on everyone else. They refuse to love others, which prevents their families from achieving the happiness and the wealth they deserve. Someone's bad decisions should not be a cause for you to worry. You do not need to stop; it is just another obstacle that must be overcome.

Poverty rests on the desire to become rich. Wealth rests on love and romance. Move forward in your life and do not look back.

Consider the following parable.

To ensure that all the students had learned the assignment, their teacher proposed an experiment. The students had to remember all the wrongs done to them by others. They wrote the names of the offenders on a potato, one for each person who had wronged them. Each student had to gather a sufficient amount of potatoes to be placed in a bag. Every day the students had to carry the bag everywhere they went. Some of the bags were really heavy. The students were asked to carry the bag for a week.

Of course, it was hard and uncomfortable. Moreover, while they were going through their day, the students had to keep track of the bag and remember where it was. As a consequence, they forgot about more important and relevant matters. In addition, the potatoes started to spoil and smelled unpleasant after a few days.

The experiment showed that everyone had a bag filled with sentimental, spoiled potatoes. It showed how we pay, every day, for holding on to the memories of people who wronged us. We carry around past grievances that cannot be changed.

Only forgiveness exempts us from other people's insults and the weight of their choices and gives a sense of spiritual freedom. Resentment and anger are toxins that poison us constantly and can accumulate in high doses. We think that forgiveness is a gift for the offender. It isn't. We do not realize that we win so much more by forgiving—we become free.

Often the first person you need to forgive is yourself. We blame ourselves for the harsh words and the memories of our bad deeds. We punish ourselves with guilt instead of learning to love ourselves. How can we love someone else if we treat ourselves poorly? Forgiving yourself and forgiving others are the key to freedom.

NOTES

CHAPTER 9

HOW TO MAKE MORE MONEY

In reality, we know that if we can learn to manage our money, we can also grow and learn to make more as well.

1. How much money would you like to earn per month in three years?

2. What to do?

3. How to remove self-limitations.

4. Three spheres of development.

5. How to manage your time.

6. Wisdom.

7. Investment in your future.

8. List of people who are where you want to be.

9. Fear.

10. Four unique books.

11. Characteristics you need to be successful.

HOW MUCH MONEY WOULD YOU LIKE TO EARN PER MONTH IN THREE YEARS?

Seriously think about the amount you aspire to and write down your answer below.

_____

_____

_____

_____

_____

_____

There are two types of people based on how differently they talk and how differently they behave when they set goals and begin to seek them.

The first type oconsists of people who look at their wages, their abilities, and where they are at the present moment. Then they evaluate their chances on the basis of their current situation. They look up, see how far they need to go, and then give up at once. It seems to them that the climb is impossible. So do the losers . . . and those who have no dreams.

The second type consists of people who are more motivated and experienced. The first type consists of people who look at themselves, and their own capabilities, at the present time. The second type consists of people who look at persons who have already achieved success and who are already where they want to be. A successful person has more chances, more opportunities, more acquaintances, more partners, and more self-confidence.

This second type of person achieves more significant results than novices. Experienced people communicate with those who have self-confidence and perseverance, and they get positive results. In the first case, people look at a successful person and think, *Wow, how can I get there?!* The people watching in the second case are looking at a successful person and imagining that they are already there, because going down is always easier than climbing up. So they gain confidence.

When persons look ahead, they see all the things that are in their sight. If they go outside and see the front of a multistory building, it can be an obstacle. It is hiding everything that is behind it. Even a single tree or a car can be a barrier beyond which you will not see your goal. If you go to the twentieth floor, has your field of vision increased? How about if you fly on a plane?

Remember the conclusion: the level of personal development of the individual determines the achievement of set goals. For people who have not put in the effort to learn and expand their minds, even small goals may be unattainable, and they do not see the big goal at all. Education broadens your field of view, raises the bar of your ability, and increases the level of your goals.

When you look down, you can see obstacles and look for options to overcome them. It is easier for you to navigate and evaluate. If a person has only a small goal, then any obstacle can obscure the visibility of the goal, and it will seem elusive. Such persons no longer see their own goal: the obstacle obscures it, because the goal is very small.

On the basis of this, let's take the figure that you wrote down as your desired income in three years and multiply it by two. You may think it's too much. But, nevertheless, let's do so. You know what happens when you set a big goal? You will be able to see your goal through any obstacle. Now you can see your goal and the obstacle. If you believe in yourself, and in your strength, then the goal will be quite real for you.

WHAT TO DO?

Never let success get to your head and
never let failure get to your heart.
~DRAKE

There is a difference between being confident and being arrogant. Everyone has special skills and knowledge, and we all have the capacity to learn more. So what can we do to ensure we are successful and working towards our goals?

1. Be confident.

2. Do not be the fox.

3. Surround yourself with lions.

BE CONFIDENT

You will probably agree that today it is not enough to be professional, not enough to be talented, and not enough to be smart. These qualities are necessary, and you need to learn to use them in life. For this to work, develop self-confidence, work on yourself, and strive to improve your level of development. Try to think about it every day.

If you perform your work well, study diligently, and read a lot, and you still are not confident in yourself, all your positive qualities will not be enough. People will be able to feel your lack of confidence. Self-confidence is a quality that will help you realize your potential. If you decide to do something, do not hesitate. Act confidently, because life loves strong and confident people.

Nick Vujicic, the renowned motivational speaker and author, once said that indecision is a decision. That is so true.

Attempt everything, or anything, and try to do something, but do not flounder in inaction. So what if you lost some money; perhaps you gained invaluable experience in the process. Besides, according to the philosophy of Thomas Edison, you now know five hundred roads that you do not need to travel! All that we do, all our mistakes and achievements, are a priceless experience which helps us to move forward faster.

DO NOT BE THE FOX

There are a few things you should know. If you do not increase your level of development, you will find it difficult to become rich. Under certain circumstances, you can get rich at the time, but you can also lose your wealth very quickly. To save the wealth, you need to have a comprehensive knowledge.

What features or capabilities characterize a fox? Cunningness, resourcefulness, maybe even deceptiveness?

There are people with such qualities. Under normal circumstances, they seem quite friendly. But if they become angry, they lose all control. They tend to remember all the wrongs done to them many years ago. In their private lives, they pretend to love, trying to seem as if they are head over heels in love. However, in real life, they do not love and are only playing the role of Romeo.

If such persons succeed, they put their noses up in the air and cease to notice the people they used to associate with. If their situation goes bad, they become the embodiment of kindness and understanding.

When they are informed about the failures of friends or relatives, they straighten their shoulders and say with malice, "I told them that's what would happen, so be it!"

You have probably noticed that when you are doing well, some of your relatives applaud and say, "Well done!" They say that they knew you were a good, capable man. However, if you suddenly slip or hit bad times, these same people will say that you were frivolous or not very capable, and that was why nothing was working for you. These are the types of people who are like the fox.

When you tell them about someone else's misfortune, they begin to smile. When they hear about someone else's success, that smile becomes a frown. They do not like it when other people are more successful than they are.

The author M. S. Norbekov said, "If someone will find out that you are immortal, then no matter what, they will kill you, and will study your cells in a lab, so they can become immortal themselves."

Never be the fox. Never use compliments to solve your problems. Speak from the heart, no matter whether the person you are dealing with has done any favors for you. Do not cheat others and do not be fooled by others. If you notice the slightest quality of a fox in a partner or colleague, get rid of such persons. Like weeds, they will destroy all of your sincerity and your existence.

If you have potted plants at home and they have turned yellow and wilted, what do you do? Do you paint the flowers so they look beautiful and attractive? Or do you water and care for them? Of course, you will water and care for them.

There is no need to "artificially paint" away the features of a fox. Instead try to work with these qualities in yourself, gradually eliminating them.

SURROUND YOURSELF WITH LIONS

In other words, surround yourself with strong, motivated, successful people. They infect you with their success, inspire you by their example, and imbue you with their positive qualities.

Scientists conducted an experiment in which they placed two rats in different cages. One had a comfortable, carefree life. It was fed and watered, and the cage was regularly cleaned. The second rat had to find its own food.

After a hundred days, the scientists checked the development of the rats' brain cells. The second rat, which had to fend for itself, showed a level of brain cell development 150 percent higher than the first rat, which had been coddled and cared for.

Then, they changed the rats' places. After the same amount of time elapsed, they checked their development again. Now, the first rat's thinking level was high, and the second rat's thinking level was back to the previous state. Obviously, when there is nothing to strive for, development is hampered.

Therefore, if you surround yourself with grumblers, whiners, and losers, you will eventually become the same. However, if you surround yourself with strong, purposeful, self-confident, and successful people, you will have the opportunity to be the same.

HOW TO REMOVE SELF-LIMITATIONS

Self-limitations are divided into three types:

1. Delay (principle of seventy-two hours).

2. Blame.

3. Justification.

DELAY (PRINCIPLE OF SEVENTY-TWO HOURS)

Only 2 percent of all people achieve their dreams. Do you know why this happens? Our brain has several layers of memory that store information.

_____1

_____2

_____3

The uppermost layer is RAM (random-access memory), which gets the latest information. You do not consider how it should be processed. People sometimes use this information intuitively.

Do you have an idea that you are really excited about? For the first three days, you believe that you can implement it. Then, after three days (seventy-two hours), it begins to slowly decline in activity because the information that gave rise to the idea goes to the second layer.

The first layer stores information that you repeat on a daily basis. The second layer is the information that you use less frequently.

For example, say that you and your friends went on vacation a week ago and relaxed on the beach. There, you met a man who was also on vacation. When you try to remember him, you cannot think of his name. If something comes up and you have a need to remember his name, you ask your friends because you have already forgotten and indeed can barely remember what he looked like.

Then the following happens. After a while, if you do not use the information, it goes to the third layer. This is long-term memory. This layer stores the information you use very rarely. It can be stored there for years.

For example, let's say you want to do something and say to yourself, "I'll do it someday." Gradually, this information is "demoted" and enters the next layer. You do not think about it. Then you find out that someone else has implemented your idea. It immediately comes to your mind that you had the same idea and wanted to do it, too.

Perhaps you heard some anecdote or parable, but it is not retold, and you gradually forget it. Maybe this takes two to three years. Suddenly, while visiting old friends, someone tells this anecdote, and you suddenly remember it.

Then the information goes into the next layer. Now all that you can do is dream about your idea, because in real life you have not already accomplished it.

To keep this from happening, every seventy-two hours you need to review your plans—to remember all your ideas, to start the implementation of the plans, and to take at least the first steps towards achieving your goals. This principle should accompany you for life. Your dreams will come true because the information will be in the first storage layer. This will help the seventh layer, the formation of relevant events. The sixth layer, an intuitive selection and attraction of the people who will help you to do this, will also come into play.

The first layer of your memory, and indeed the human brain, is like a radio station. It receives and distributes thought waves. For example, have you ever thought of someone and immediately receive a call from that person, as if he or she were reading your mind?

Therefore, try to begin to implement all your plans as soon as possible, even if difficulties arise. Success depends on this. Do not postpone your plans because of emerging obstacles. Remember this: what comes easily is cheaply valued. Plan specific results and consistently work towards your goal. Success seeks those who work on their dreams despite the many challenges they may face.

As you can see from the description of memory layers, your mind is like a computer's memory. It contains different levels, with RAM being the first level. You will learn how to properly use all the layers of your memory, and you will learn to memorize necessary information and recall the right information at the right time. It is a very important skill to optimally organize your memories and not forget any of the things that can be useful later.

In training, I sometimes cite examples that I heard in the fourth grade or relate what an instructor told me ten years ago. This is due to the fact I have a memorization system that works. Therefore, when I speak or present, I do not prepare at home. I just go on stage and talk.

If you thoroughly prepare and learn everything, then you're likely to go out on stage and talk like a parrot. You will not actually say anything useful or inspiring. Why do so many agents and sellers talk so persuasively and professionally, but nobody buys anything from them? It is because they are 90 percent speech, but only 10 percent feeling.

It should be the exact opposite. Sincere feelings are the most important, so they should be 90 percent of any presentation. The words should only be 10 percent. When I am training, I try to speak sincerely from the heart. It is very important to be honest because people feel your emotional state. The best form of training is 98 percent personal example, and only 2 percent explanation.

We need to constantly train our minds. Constant exercise develops our thinking, memory, and intuition. It is necessary to develop self-confidence, looseness, and a feeling of self-esteem. Every day you need to learn and exercise your mind.

Our experience tells us that for every seventeen negative responses we hear, we only hear and process one that is positive. The brain remembers eleven examples of the negative responses, and only one that is positive. That is an impressive ratio. There is a special program that helps to mix all memory layers. Therefore, I can very easily remember everything needed for my training and seminars. This is because I have studied and know the mechanisms that help store the necessary information in my memory.

BLAME

Most people blame their misfortunes on everyone but themselves. They are looking for a cause in the external environment, in the circumstances, in an unfavorable alignment of the stars, but not within themselves.

When I traveled frequently from Tajikistan to different Russian cities, my luggage was constantly checked by the authorities. Of course, it was insulting when they came into the car and checked only my luggage. Once, I was checked thirteen times! In the end, I grew tired of this and just told the policeman, "Here, on the top shelf, is my suitcase. Get it and check it yourself."

When I started to analyze the situation later, I realized that the reason for my situation existed somewhere in me. It is nobody else's fault when someone treats us that way. Do not blame the whole world. First of all, blame yourself, because the reason lies within us.

Remember one rule: never blame the state or the laws, your relatives, or your friends—nobody. The Bible says in Matthew 7:1, "Judge not, that ye be not judged." If you blame life, then life starts to blame you. Your thoughts, emotions, and attitude towards someone else will eventually return.

It's easy to blame someone or something else. For this, a great mind is not necessary. It is human nature to blame someone rather than yourself.

If these accusations are made when the other person is present, be prepared to hear that person's accusations in response. Any condemnation will cause a reaction. It is better to try to understand the person, because it will affect your relationship and also create the desire to reciprocate within the other person. Any understanding that creates fellowship and joint action is the key to future success.

So be strong, and look for the cause of your failure within yourself. Correct your deficiencies, use your strengths, and do not repeat old mistakes. Constantly continue to learn and raise your level of development. Remember what Confucius said, "Don't complain about the snow on your neighbor's roof when your own doorstep is unclean."

JUSTIFICATION

You can justify anything: betrayal, deceit, envy, even an unseemly act. The world is full of excuses, and people manage to come up with new ones. However, remember this: if you're able to justify your unfavorable position, that means that you will never fix it.

Do not look for excuses for your poverty, or you will always be poor. Do not look for excuses for your failures, or you will remain a loser. Do not look for excuses with regard to family problems; otherwise, you will never achieve harmony in your family. Do not look for excuses, but try to achieve results. No excuse can replace the results.

People justify things in order to make life easier, not better. When you stop making excuses, you cease shifting your responsibility for your position onto others. Then you begin to realize that the cause of all your troubles rests within yourself. When you stop making excuses, you change your life and gain self-confidence.

Your weakness is the main reason for your failure. Work on yourself, because you yourself are the source of all your victories and your defeats. All victories start with victories over yourself.

THREE SPHERES OF SELF-DEVELOPMENT

1. Spiritual.

2. Physical.

3. Mental.

SPIRITUAL

We understand the spiritual growth in each of us in our own way. But we all agree that it is impossible to imagine our lives without the spiritual sphere. Whether we want it or not, the spiritual component, as well as the material component, is an integral part of our lives. They are two sides of the same coin. And I know one thing. If you put your strength, energy, and sense into the spiritual world, everything comes back to you in an even greater amount. Do not deny the real world in which you live. The spiritual and the material are closely linked. They serve as a sustainable support just as our two legs support our physical bodies. It is impossible to stand on one leg for very long, regardless of how strong that leg is!

PHYSICAL

Physical development is your health. Always find time when you are young to pray to God. Pray for good health, love, and prosperity.

Do you know why old people start to pray? Because they are afraid. They are afraid of illness, loneliness, and being misunderstood. I was recently very pleased to see a lot of young people in the mosques, churches, and temples. Always find time for spirituality.

Similarly, take time to exercise your body. Select any kind of sport. It is desirable to have more than one, because your physical condition determines the speed of your thinking.

Consider engaging in and playing team sports like football, volleyball, or basketball. If the body is weak, the brain is the same. Nobody who is sluggish has a sharp mind. And if you eat sweets and fatty foods every day and do not exercise, over time you will gain weight. Your weight gain will inevitably lead to health problems. Then, for sure, you will not be able to pursue your lofty goals.

MENTAL

You need to train your mind. I will repeat it once again: the best investment is an investment in yourself, in your intelligence. It cannot be compared with anything else. Your mind is an instrument of labor on which your level of success or failure depends.

Attend all the training that you can. Read more books to increase your intellectual level. Strengthen your memory by studying foreign languages. Develop your talents. Obtain the appropriate education to enhance your abilities. Make time for physical exercise and sports. Work towards your goals and enjoy life. Do these things, and you will not feel tired.

How may you relax from life? Why do people come home from work and say that they are tired and need a rest? Because their work does not bring them joy and they do not realize their potential. Joyless work turns a job into a difficult obligation and an unpleasant duty. Make sure your work brings you pleasure, and it will be a source of happiness and energy.

HOW TO MANAGE YOUR TIME

A man who dares to waste one hour of time
has not discovered the value of life.
~ CHARLES DARWIN

Do you know why people have lost confidence in the future and have anxiety?

Everything seems to be okay. Their children are healthy, they make good money, and they have a roof over their head, yet the anxiety still remains. That's because they do not know how to manage their time. They are always in a hurry, and they are constantly in a nervous state.

Learn to manage time properly. Most people feel there is

a constant shortage of time. If there were forty-eight hours in a day, they would still not have enough time to do everything.

Sometimes people just fixate on the fact that they do not have enough time. They always think they are late and cannot meet required deadlines. Do not focus your attention on time. Just remember when you were a child and had the feeling that time was endless. Do you remember the summer break from school, when for three months you could do what you wanted? While you were in school, those forty-five minutes of class seemed like an eternity. But during the five-minute break between your classes, you had enough time to run, play, and goof off in the hallway.

Give your body a chance to rejuvenate, and it will give you extra time. Learn to manage time properly.

Skillful management and distribution of your time are the key to success and the only way to achieve higher goals. Time is the only category that we cannot return.

Consider this story about time.

Imagine that there is a bank that credits your account with $86,400 every morning and that every evening withdraws anything left over that you did not use during the day. What would you do? Of course, you would take every last penny from your account each day.

Each of us has such a bank. Every morning, the bank puts into our account 86,400 seconds. Every night, the bank removes anything left in our account. What is left refers to the loss of time that has not been used for something good. This bank does not allow saving and does not let us keep leftovers. Every day we open a new account, and every night we give back the balance we did not use. If you do not use the deposit during the day, this is your loss. Nothing can bring it back, nothing can be changed, and there is no transfer of balances for tomorrow.

We can only live on today's deposit. It is better to spend as much as possible on your health, your happiness, and your success. Time is running. Use the maximum you can during the day. You can realistically feel and sense the price of time.

All students will tell how much a year of study is worth when they are passing their classes.

Any mother will tell you how much the first month of a child's life is worth in the month in which she gave birth.

Anyone who survives an accident can say how much one second is worth.

Anyone in love can tell how long an hour of waiting seems before a date with his or her beloved.

All champions will tell you how much it costs for that one-hundredth of a second which put them up on a podium.

Time waits for no one. Therefore, it would be nice to learn to appreciate the time, every moment, especially when you are with someone near and dear.

Time is the only thing that has an irreplaceable value. Nothing is given to us so easily. Time does not cost that much, yet nothing is so expensive. Time waits for no one.

Yesterday is history, tomorrow is a mystery, and today is a gift—that is why it is called the present.

WISDOM

1. Life experience.

2. The life of others.
   A. Books and reading.
   B. Wisdom and folly.
   C. Observation.

You will be very rich if you become wise. To do this, you need to remember the rules which will lead you down the road of wisdom.

LIFE EXPERIENCE

Use your own life experiences. Errors we make are too expensive to repeat them, so learn from them. Think about possibilities of how to correct them and to eliminate their effects. Identify your weaknesses which lead to negative results so that you can get rid of them. Be sure to think about your positive results and understand how you achieved them. Use your achievements for future victories.

THE LIFE OF OTHERS

Study the lives and experiences of other people. It is not necessary to learn only from your mistakes. Wise people learn the most from the mistakes that others have made. This point is divided into several parts:

Books and Reading

It is important to read at least fifty pages per day. (It should take you about one hour.) When you have a good profession and a good salary, you are calm and confident, and it will be much easier for you to devote time to reading books, newspapers, or magazines.

You may have had a lot of intellectual activity when you were younger, studying numerous subjects even during the night, but this decreases as you age. Don't rely on lightweight newspaper reading, because you will stop training your brain to retain information and your ability to learn will gradually decrease. You need to study and to train your brain; otherwise, your ability to learn will gradually decline.

All our thoughts and ideas are the result of the books we read and the life experiences we have. So read more. In this case, select literature that requires considerable intellectual effort. Just as exercise keeps you in good physical shape, reading books will maintain good intellectual shape. Better to skip breakfast, lunch, or dinner than to skip working on yourself.

Relaxation for many revolves around sitting in a cafe and having fun but pointless conversations. They earn money to spend on useless activities, and then they earn money over again. And so the circle continues. Wouldn't it be more useful to invest that money in their own education?

If you are not investing in yourself, you will not achieve anything. Therefore, I repeat—it is better to skip breakfast, lunch, or dinner than to skip working on yourself.

Wisdom and Folly

You may ask, "Why do I need to study the stupidity of people?" The answer is very simple. Wisdom advises how to do it. To do this, read the quotes of great people. Stupidity shows you what not to do.

Once a wise man was asked why he was so polite. He said, "I learned from impolite people. What they did, I tried not to do."

Observation

Be attentive and observant. Pay particular attention to those who have both won—and lost—in life. Try to understand the reasons why one person won, but the other person lost. Analyze their errors and omissions, learn from their positive experiences, and draw your own conclusions. Use the experiences of others to achieve your goals and realize your dreams.

INVESTMENT IN YOUR FUTURE

These three things all impact your life . . . whether you realize or not.

1. Finance.
2. Time.
3. Effort.

FINANCE

Do not spare money on yourself. The higher you value yourself, the more you will achieve. Do not focus your attention on high prices. If you see a nice expensive suit, believe that you are worthy of it. Luxury and quality things will give you confidence and positive energy.

TIME

Do not hesitate to spare time for yourself. Spread it around so that every day you can have time for exercise, reading a book, and relaxing in nature.

EFFORT

Remember that with no effort, you will achieve nothing and reach none of your goals. It makes no sense to hope for an easy victory and fast results.

It has long been known that talent is 90 percent labor and patience, only 10 percent ability. Most efforts are put into the development of your abilities. As Leo Tolstoy said, "A good life is given only to those who make efforts to achieve it." Your efforts in the present will determine your position in the future.

LIST OF PEOPLE WHO ARE WHERE YOU WANT TO BE

Write a list of ten people with whom you communicate often and spend most of your time.

1. ——————————————————————

2. ——————————————————————

3. ——————————————————————

4. _____
5. _____
6. _____
7. _____
8. _____
9. _____
10. _____

Now think about the fact that in five to seven years, you will become the same as they are. Your environment affects you and shapes your future.

Now make a list of ten people who are where you wish to be in your finances and in your career.

1. _____
2. _____
3. _____
4. _____
5. _____
6. _____
7. _____
8. _____
9. _____
10. _____

By communicating with successful people, you will learn from them and will absorb some of their experience. Eliminate the shortcomings that prevent you from moving forward. Gain skills which will help you achieve your goal, and gradually you will be as successful as they are.

Only, of course, if you want to.

FEAR

1. Poverty.

2. Old Age.

3. Disease.

4. Love Lost.

5. Critics.

6. Death.

7. Unknown.

Fear prevents us from achieving our goals. It paralyzes our will, deprives us of our confidence, and saps our strength. Fear often causes us to be content with what we have, forcing us to give up our dreams.

Fear of poverty leads us into working at a job we do not like, doing work we do not like, even communicating with uninteresting people. We become afraid to change anything in our lives. As we age, we begin to fear the coming of old age and sickness. Fear by itself seems like a disease and often leads to painful conditions.

Is it necessary to be afraid of the inevitable? Each age has its charms and advantages. Fear does not give us anything positive; it only steals the strength and energy needed to realize our plans. Never be afraid of criticism. It helps you to correct your mistakes and get rid of your shortcomings. It is better to avoid flattery. It distorts the perception of yourself and fuels an excessive ego.

Fear is not an organ; it does not exist. It is just a state of mind, and it can be changed. Fear appears when indecision is reinforced in your mind. It joins the mind and starts to bear the fruit of doubt. This "couple," indecision and doubt, generates fear and paralyzes the will to act. You want to do something and cannot. Your desires do not coincide with your actions and, even more so, with the results.

To get rid of fear, try to develop a strong resolve. Do not bypass the problem. Do not look for the easiest way to get away from it. Focus on the solution. It's like placing small blocks on each other, climbing on them higher and higher. Then, little by little, step-by-step, you will rise above a seemingly unsolvable problem. One day, you will simply see that you are standing above it.

All people have a fear of death. Death is inevitable. There will come a day when our names will not be repeated every day and when we have nobody waiting. But one thing will remain. Our kindness. Good, made by our hands, will never die.

One good way to conquer death is to share all that you have. Share your love, your time, your capabilities, your money, your knowledge, and everything you have. Then death will have nothing to take away from you.

People are afraid of death because they do not have the time to live. Life is beautiful. If we learn to live well, then we have no reason to fear death.

Do not be afraid of the unknown, because such fear prevents you from moving forward. Remember that your thoughts and feelings determine your future.

What happens when we are afraid to lose? Often, we lose when we are afraid to get sick, which in turn makes us ill. When we are afraid of problems, and they just keep piling on us, making us more afraid.

Do not concentrate on your fears. They will pull you back and deprive you of hope.

Charge yourself with positive energy and think about health, if you want to be healthy. Think about wealth, if you want to become rich. Think about love, if you want to be loved. Do not focus on what you do not want. Focus on your desires and dreams. This will generate the conditions necessary for their creation.

FOUR UNIQUE BOOKS

1. *Book of Success.*
2. *Book of Wisdom.*
3. *Book of Victories.*
4. *Book of Ideas.*

These are four unique books that are necessary for your success. These books will be written about your success in life, about your small and large victories, about wise advice which accompanied you in life, and about your good ideas that still need implementation.

Take four notebooks or notepads and write on each of them the name of the book: *Book of Success, Book of Wisdom, Book of Victories,* and *Book of Ideas.* Write down all your thoughts and actions that match the topics of these books. It is best to do it on a daily basis, analyzing the past day and summing up the results. This will discipline you, allow you to plan your business for the next day, and maintain a positive attitude.

In *The Book of Success*, write down your accomplishments and positive results. Express everything in detail, focusing on why you have achieved success. You may describe your feelings and the joy you received from success. When difficulties appear in your life, reread these records, remembering your successes and achievements. They will inspire you to go forward, because you will again believe that you will ultimately succeed.

The Book of Wisdom is also very important. In it write quotes and sayings of the sages and famous people which will help guide you in life. They will help you to overcome obstacles and inspire you to victory. By rereading this book, you will be able to avoid making many mistakes and deal wisely and effectively with difficult problems.

The Book of Victories is about your victories: overcoming obstacles, solving difficult problems, achieving goals, and getting rid of disturbing flaws. All of these are your victories. The most important victory is a victory over yourself, over your weaknesses, and it will help you realize your most cherished dreams.

In the *Book of Ideas*, write down all your ideas that are worthy of implementation. Good ideas tend to appear suddenly in your mind. If they are not written down immediately, they are forgotten very quickly. How many people have missed the chance to become successful only because they did not write an idea that suddenly came to their mind? You only remember your idea when it is implemented by someone else. So do not be lazy. Writing down your ideas in your notebook is necessary, even if you are busy with something else or if the idea suddenly comes to you in the middle of the night. One good idea can make you rich.

CHARACTERISTICS YOU NEED TO BE SUCCESSFUL

1. Commitment.

2. Self-confidence.

3. The habit of saving money.

4. Initiative and leadership.

5. Imagination.

6. Enthusiasm.

7. Self-control.

8. The habit of doing more than expected.

9. An interesting personality.

10. The accuracy of thought.

11. Ability to concentrate.

12. Communication skills.

13. Learning from failures.

14. Tolerance.

15. The application of the Golden Rule.

Once a wise man stood in front of his students. He took a large glass jar and filled it to the brim with big stones. Doing this, he asked the students whether the jar was full. They all said that yes, it was full.

Then the sage took a box of pebbles and poured them into the jar. He gently shook the jar a few times. The pebbles rolled into the spaces between the large stones and filled them. The sage asked his students again, if the jar was full. They again confirmed that it was full.

Finally, the wise man picked up a box of sand and poured its contents into the same vessel. The sand, of course, filled the last gaps between the stones.

Now the sage turned to his students, and said, "I would like you to look at this vessel of life. The large stones represent the important things in your life. Your way of life, your faith, your family, your loved ones, your health, and your children. With these things, even if you have nothing else, your life will always be full."

He held up the vessel for the students to see and continued, "The small stones are less important things, such as work, your home, or your hobby. The sand, a vital detail, is the daily bustle. If you fill your containers with sand at the beginning, there is no room for larger stones. It is the same in life: if you spend all your energy on the small things, there is nothing left for your large and important affairs. Therefore, pay attention primarily to the important things, find time for your children and your loved ones, and take care of your health."

You still have enough time for work, for home, for celebrations, and everything else. Attend to the big rocks only since they have a price: everything else is only sand.

Notes

CHAPTER 10

PHILOSOPHY OF THE ANT

People have long known that ants have a clear organization of teamwork and order in their lives. They are admired for their diligence and patience. It is in the harmony of nature that people try to find answers to many questions of the universe, and ants have always served as an example for humans because of their dedication and perseverance.

Humans have learned that ants are not afraid of obstacles, believe in themselves, and achieve their goals. There are a lot of quotes and sayings about ants. Here are some of them:

Ants work together, and shall overcome the lion. ("When many work together for a goal, great things may be accomplished. It is said a lion cub was killed by a single colony of ants.")
~ SASKYA PANDITA

Go to the ant, lazy, learn from him prudence. No preacher is more eloquent than an ant, who lives without uttering a

*sound. The ant is weak, but breaks the stone down.
The ant has a small body, but is great in results
(a little body often harbors a great soul).*

An ant is happy to another ant.
~ POLISH PROVERB

*An ant has a head the size of a millet seed, and the mind is a
closet. The ant is small, and digs in the mountain.
Go to the ant, thou sluggard; consider her ways, and be wise.
Which having no guide, overseer, or ruler. Provideth her meat
in the summer, and gathereth her food in the harvest.*
~ PROVERBS 6:6–8

*The ants are a people not strong, yet they prepare their meat in
the summer. The colonies are but a feeble folk, yet make they
their houses in the rocks.*
~ PROVERBS 30:25–26

*The ant is not only feelings,
but also the mind, intellect, memory.*
~ CICERO

*If someone could take a look from the sky down to the earth,
what would be the difference between the work he noticed
people on the one hand, bees and ants—the other?*
~ CELSUS

*[T]he smallest in size are often the most wonderful—
the works of ants and bees astonishing us more
than the huge bodies of whales.*
~ ST. AUGUSTINE (BRACKETS MINE)

*The object of course is small, but do not be ashamed.
The ant, how it seems fit to notify us it is the
King of Reason and infinitely wise.*
~ V. GULD

We also tried to understand the life of ants and formulate the principles that will help many to realize their dreams. It is nature that gives us startling examples of dedication and perseverance. This is the philosophy of the ant, which is the whole wisdom of nature. So here are these principles:

In ancient times, wise men and advisors would share how life works imperfectly. Things *will* fall apart. To rebuild their lives, they should follow the example of the ants.

The ant never gives up.

Ants teach each other; the older and more experienced teach the younger ones.

The ants go to their goal, not noticing the obstacles.

Ants show other ants the shortest path to the goal. Ants always help each other in difficult situations.

Ants, however far they may go, always return home.

The stimulus for ants is the needs of the family.

The actions of each ant are aimed at ensuring the well-being of the family.

Ants take up any job if it is necessary for the family.

Ants gather food in an amount many times greater than their personal needs. This shows concern for others.

Ants do the work which at first glance seems impossible.

Ants perform set tasks flawlessly.

Ants combine their efforts on difficult tasks to solve problems.

Ants' objectives are achieved only by concerted action. Consistency in action is a necessary condition for success.

Ants take care of each other on the basis of reciprocity and even reward.

Ants are very hardworking and work from early morning until late evening.

Ants have surpassed all in the precise organization of labor.

For each ant, there is a choice of activities and the opportunity to display initiative.

Initiative is encouraged among ants and is the basis of the existence of the anthill.

Victory in the ant family depends on the ability to unite the target groups during battles.

Leaders manage and guide other ants.

The collective strength of each ant increases.

The main principle of the life of ants is one for all and all for one.

Ants do not pass by those in need of help.

You have a lot to learn from ants, particularly with regard to the organization of teamwork.

At all times, the ant is a symbol of hard work and patience.

After an unsuccessful attempt, ants start over, and do so many times until they win.

Coherent teamwork allows the ants to perform the most difficult, almost impossible task.

In overcoming difficulties, ants have no equal.

Each ant is disciplined and persistent in carrying out its duties.

Ants live in harmony with nature.

Notes

_____

_____

_____

_____

_____

_____

_____

_____

_____

_____

_____

_____

_____

_____

_____

_____

_____

_____

_____

_____

_____

_____

_____

_____

_____

Dear Reader,

Thank you for finishing this book. Well done! However, all the knowledge contained in this book is theory, and the theory provides a success rate of only 10 to 30 percent. True understanding of this book provides you with both the principles and the guidelines to utilize the knowledge in the book. Understanding the principles and the guidelines will help you put into practice what you have learned, which leads to success.

Please instill in your mind an antlike philosophy and use the rules that we have learned from the observation of these insects. They are the true symbol of hard work, perseverance, and determination. I use *The Philosophy of the Ant* throughout my book series to help you as you explore the dedication of the ant. I advise you to find a picture or a drawing of an ant. Hang it on the wall so that it will remind you about the ants' will and perseverance in achieving their goals, and about the kindness and mutual aid which fills the life of an ant. And about the wisdom of nature, which is our main mentor.

If you have finished reading this book, then we share something in common. We have common views and aspirations. I want success for you. I know that you, too, can achieve a lot in your life.

I wrote this book, as your true servant, with one goal—that all persons who hold this book in their hands live such a life that when they look back, they will want to live their life over again because they were able realize all their dreams. And, by the end of their life, they will have shared their experiences with their children, grandchildren and great-grandchildren.

Email your comments or suggestions to admin@worldpreneur.com. We are happy for you to share your opinions or express criticism, because only readers determine the value of any book.

Sincerely,
S. Davlatov

About the Author

Saidmurod Davlatov

 Saidmurod Davlatov is a global author and entrepreneur with a mission to help others succeed. His books have sold millions of copies across the world, and this groundbreaking book, *Me and Money*, helps people think differently about their relationship with wealth.

Me and Money has already sold hundreds of thousands of copies. As of 2016, the *Me and Money* series consists of six books on topics such as financial and money management, business strategy, relationship development, and network marketing, with two more books awaiting publication. In addition, Said has also written a children's book and created a workshop to develop financial literacy and entrepreneurial aspirations for children ages six to twelve.

Said was born in Tajikistan. The youngest of ten children, he lost his father when he was just one year old. When Said was eight, his mother experienced financial hardship but wanted the best for him, so she sent him to live with his mentor, who educated him on life and business, and laid the foundation of his character. These experiences shaped his life and fueled his desire to give back.

After graduating from high school with honors, Said began his university education. When civil war erupted in Tajikistan, he had no time and no money to study. After quitting three institutes, he moved to Moscow to work.

Said enrolled in the Princes Shcherbatov Interethnic Academy of Arts and Natural Sciences (IAANS) in Moscow, where he was awarded his PhD.

He also completed training with Mirzakarim Norbekov, founder of the Institute of Human Self-Healing. He began a mentorship with Bodo Schafer, a top financial consultant in Europe, and learned principles that changed his mind-set and his life.

Since then, Said has trained with world-renowned entrepreneurs, businessmen, and personal development coaches Stephen Covey, Brian Tracy, Tetsuo Yasuyi, Richard Branson, and Smiljan Mori.

Throughout his education and training, Said successfully launched and managed more than fifty businesses in a variety of industries, including construction, food services, retail services, manufacturing, travel and tourism, agriculture, and real estate, among others.

He created SAMO, the International Center for Human Development, to help others by educating them on financial management, health and fitness, and relationship development. He organizes and teaches a variety of workshops and seminars designed to improve financial knowledge, create business strategy, enhance leadership and management techniques, as well as develop an integrative approach to body, mind, and spirit.

Despite his busy schedule as a husband, father, entrepreneur, and business coach/mentor, Said continues his own self-improvement journey by investing in education and mentorships with top business and personal development coaches.

In his free time, he enjoys spending time with his family, composing, and singing.

NOTES

NOTES

NOTES

NOTES

NOTES

NOTES

NOTES

NOTES

NOTES

NOTES

www.ingramcontent.com/pod-product-compliance
Lightning Source LLC
Jackson TN
JSHW011949131224
75386JS00042B/1625

* 9 7 8 1 9 4 5 5 0 7 6 6 3 *